Nothing's Impossible

Nothing's Impossible

The Peter Sampson Story

Sharing the wonder of wildlife;
protection is our passion

Keep Happy, Keep Smiling

First published in 2025 by Tim Ewbank
in partnership with Whitefox Publishing

www.wearewhitefox.com

Copyright © Tim Ewbank, 2025

EU GPSR Authorised Representative
LOGOS EUROPE, 9 rue Nicolas Poussin,
17000, LA ROCHELLE, France

E-mail: Contact@logoseurope.eu

ISBN 978-1-917523-41-7
Also available as an eBook
ISBN 978-1-917523-42-4

Tim Ewbank asserts the moral right
to be identified as the author of this work.

All rights reserved. No part of this publication
may be reproduced, stored in a retrieval system or
transmitted in any form or by any means, electronic,
mechanical, photocopying, recording or
otherwise, without prior written permission of the author.

While every effort has been made to trace the owners of copyright
material reproduced herein, the author would like to apologise for any
omissions and will be pleased to incorporate missing
acknowledgements in any future editions.

All photographs and illustrations in this book
© Peter Sampson

Designed and typeset by Typo•glyphix
Cover design by Emma Ewbank
Colour reproduction by Rhapsody Media
Project management by Whitefox

For my family and the wonder of wildlife
– **Peter**

Foreword	ix
Preface	xi
CHAPTER ONE **Bobby the Lion**	1
CHAPTER TWO **War Baby**	5
CHAPTER THREE **The Apprentice**	19
CHAPTER FOUR **On Track**	29
CHAPTER FIVE **Wheels in Motion**	53
CHAPTER SIX **Coast to Coast**	71

CHAPTER SEVEN
Animal Instinct 91

CHAPTER EIGHT
Welcome to Paradise 103

CHAPTER NINE
A Rocky Road to Tiger Love 111

CHAPTER TEN
Claws Out at Marley Farm 131

CHAPTER ELEVEN
Well Bred 151

CHAPTER TWELVE
White Lions 167

CHAPTER THIRTEEN
Cheetahs 175

CHAPTER FOURTEEN
Bisa and Zara – Gifts to Uganda 181

CHAPTER FIFTEEN
Big Cats in Crisis 189

CHAPTER 16
A Myriad of Memories and Magical Moments 195

Acknowledgements 203
About Tim Ewbank 205
About Hertfordshire Zoo and The Big Cat Sanctuary 207

Peter has led a fascinating and varied life successfully achieving many things people can only dream about. I think probably his greatest achievement is the work he is now doing in the world of conservation. With the ever-increasing human world population, the conflict between people and wildlife for living spaces is at its most crucial. Habitat loss is driving many species to the brink of extinction. It is absolutely essential that we breed in captivity critically endangered animals that have lost their home ranges. Eventually their offspring can be returned to safe habitats and once again become part of the ecosystem of life.

Peter Scott started it at Slimbridge in the fifties with waterfowl, Gerald Durrell did pioneering work at Jersey Zoo and was instrumental in getting major zoos to become involved in conservation work. Now Peter is doing tremendous work at The Big Cat Sanctuary, not only saving traumatised felines from war-torn countries, but breeding some of the very rare smaller wild cat species which people have never heard of, let alone seen!

Well done, Peter, keep up the good work, we look forward to visiting again soon.

– David Mills MBE and Dame Judi Dench

David Mills MBE, the British Wildlife Centre

There are very few people in life who have made a success of three very diverse careers. Peter Charles Sampson is one – as a speedway rider, as a bus and coach operator, as a dedicated conservationist, a tireless fundraiser for wildlife, founder of The Big Cat Sanctuary and the Hertfordshire Zoo, and a breeder of some of the rarest and most endangered big cats on the planet.

Peter has led, and continues to lead, what by any yardstick is a most remarkable life. There can't be many men who, when asked what's new, might reply by saying the good news is that his pygmy marmosets have just given birth to two infants, his Asian short-clawed otters are doing well, construction of the new white lion complex in Kent is well under way, one of his lions has just had a tooth capped, and he was at Spurs last Saturday when Fulham managed a lucky draw.

Peter has led a life so fascinatingly out of the ordinary that it inevitably invites an endless list of questions with the answers bound to be nothing less than captivating. The lines of questioning could be varied and wide-ranging. There is plenty to ask and talk about:

So how does it feel to sit down with a fully grown 35-stone (200 kg) tiger while it nuzzles your ear and sucks your fingers and thumb?

How come you are the only man ever to deliver a white lion to the Isle of Wight?

How did you manage to take a coachload of Brits behind the Iron Curtain to Poland and back at the very height of the Cold War?

Why did you send an Amur leopard 6,000 miles from Hertfordshire to Hiroshima in Japan?

And is it true that you transported two of your own home-bred lionesses to Entebbe as a gift to Uganda at a cost to yourself of £16,000?

Was it scary driving through a bomb-torn Belfast at the height of Northern Ireland's Troubles in a white van with British number plates to collect a fully grown clouded leopard?

Why did you pay not once, but twice over to rescue a lion called Bobby?

Is it true you once beat legendary world champion Barry Briggs in a speedway race on a motorbike with no brakes?

Did you enjoy your day out at the Queen's Garden party and at Princess Eugenie's Windsor wedding?

What did you say to Boris Johnson, then Prime Minister, when he dropped in on you out of the blue?

How did you win a kiss from Miss World?

Why did the police force you to spend a night in a London theatre?

What were you doing dressed up as Lawrence of Arabia, leading a camel on a rein for quarter of a mile down Sussex country lanes?

Both directly and indirectly, in some way or another, Peter has touched many thousands of lives down the years, both human and animal, and avian and reptilian too. He has made a difference to wildlife in countless ways in dozens of countries all around the world.

No one, least of all Peter himself, could have predicted such a remarkable future for the shy boy who left school at fifteen with no academic qualifications and only a vague idea of becoming a motorbike or a car mechanic. So how did a former welder, car mechanic, coach, bus and lorry driver, travel operator, speedway rider, local councillor and liqueur ambassador become a big cat breeder known, respected and admired in zoos and wildlife parks all over the world?

There are some who will know Peter only from their schooldays when he was that cheerful young coach driver whose job was to drive pupils to and from their special needs school every day.

There are Broxbourne residents who would know him as their hard-working local councillor over a period of four years.

There are speedway fans and former riders who still only picture Peter in his leathers astride a speedway bike, fearlessly scorching around the track at speedway stadiums up and down the country.

Some will recognise Peter only from his time as the boss of a travel shop selling airline entrepreneur Freddie Laker's bargain flights to New York at £90 apiece.

Still more may just remember him in overalls carrying out an MOT service on their car on a Sunday morning.

The Amur leopard is the rarest cat on earth; there are estimated to be just sixty struggling to survive in the mountains and forests of eastern Russia. If only those pitifully few big cats could talk they would surely offer up a prayer in grateful thanks to Peter for helping to keep their magnificent species alive with his very rare success in breeding Amur leopard cubs at his Big Cat Sanctuary.

Then there's dedicated conservationist and wildlife expert Nick Marx in Cambodia, who has Peter to thank for helping to fund a prosthetic boot for an Asian elephant whose foot had been lost in a snare.

In Kenya there are rangers who know Peter as the man who funded the provision of tracking collars for lions to help in their fight against poaching.

There are 40 million people who know of Peter and his dedicated conservation work from several media platforms.

But the majority of people who have known Peter day to day over the past forty years have come to recognise him as the unassuming, genial, slim fellow full of good cheer, dressed in khaki shorts, sturdy boots and a park ranger shirt to be found unobtrusively going about his stewardship of The Big Cat Sanctuary and of Paradise Wildlife Park – now known as Hertfordshire Zoo. He is renowned for his friendly nature, which is epitomised by his signature sign-off in letters, birthday and Christmas cards, texts and emails with a cheerful 'Keep happy, keep smiling.'

To former head keeper Colin Elcombe, Peter is a role model. 'He has been a huge influence on my life. He's hard-working, a true natural leader, and as such he has influenced countless people to try and work as hard as he does. He has shaped me, and I'll always be grateful to him for teaching me how to love working hard and have a zest for life.'

To renowned sculptor and trustee of The Big Cat Sanctuary Steve Winterburn, Peter is 'like a second father', and to former Retail Ombudsman Sir Eric Peacock, who is chairman of the Trustees of The Big Cat Sanctuary and Hertfordshire Zoo, Peter is simply 'a legend in his own lifetime', an accolade emphatically endorsed by Peter's son Steve.

'A legend among men' is how Steve Sampson similarly describes his father. 'But more importantly,' he stresses, 'he's my dad, mentor, confidant, friend and hero. It's been one of my life's great pleasures working closely with my dad to deliver on his vision and dreams. He's always created a fun environment, leading from the front but in a friendly, hard-working, nothing-is-impossible way, carrying everyone with him and allowing people to flourish and become the best versions of themselves.

'It's true that Dad has tried his hand at many things, but they have always been successful, either in their own right or from learnings gained and applied. We entered the zoo industry at a time when it was filled with characters and Dad was one of those, not heeding convention and totally un-politically correct. As the renowned veterinary expert Dr Peter Scott once remarked of us after inspecting Paradise Wildlife Park: "You used to be viewed as mavericks. Now you are seen as pioneers."'

Peter's daughter Lynn says: 'Dad is often referred to as the Peter Pan of the Zoo world. That's him, never ageing, young at heart, debonair, full of energy, passionate and determined. He's the first to give you a big smile, a hug, and – in the past – a glass of Glayva! He's successful in everything he has touched, from sports to car mechanics and welding, coaches and travel to conservation, and at the age of forty changing complete direction in his life to take on, as he says, "something new that I knew nothing about", transforming Broxbourne Zoo from the "Beasts' Belsen" to Paradise Wildlife Park with exceptionally high standards in animal welfare, education and conservation, before fulfilling his dream of a private nature reserve, transforming Marley Farm into the tranquil setting of The Big Cat Sanctuary. Dad is a friend to all and he would give the last penny in his pocket and the shirt off his back. He is always happier out of the limelight but still encouraging and inspiring. He is and always will be my ultimate hero.'

Perhaps Dr James Musinguzi, Uganda's leading conservationist, sums up Peter best. As the beneficiary of two lionesses donated generously as a gift to him in his capacity as CEO of the Uganda Wildlife Conservation Education Centre, Dr James says: 'Peter's a passionate soul about wildlife conservation and a great lover of big cats. He is a remarkable achiever, an entrepreneur and motivator, a generous man with a big heart who loves his family to the fullest and wishes to see everyone happy.'

Dr James adds: 'Above all, I thank god for his life – and that we met.' There are many who would echo that – and countless wild animals, too.

CHAPTER ONE
Bobby the Lion

'He had barely enough space to turn himself around'
— *Peter Sampson*

Peter Sampson still shudders at the memory of the day he first set eyes on the lonely male lion caged in a wretchedly cramped former aviary at Broxbourne Zoo in Hertfordshire. The fully grown wild animal, incongruously named Bobby, was confined in a ramshackle pen little more than 15 feet (4.5 metres) square. To Peter, the big cat appeared to be anything but a king of the jungle.

Slumped motionless on the floor of his shabby cage, Bobby looked forlorn, lifeless and miserable as he peered at Peter through the wire netting slung between scaffolding poles which served as a barrier to his freedom. Above him, a roof consisting of a section of rusty corrugated iron and a length of old tarpaulin completed Bobby's decrepit incarceration.

Peter could not help but notice the look in the big cat's eyes of helpless resignation to his plight. His big paws were sore and worn painfully raw from pacing relentlessly up and down the same limited stretch of his pen's concrete flooring.

Peter was appalled and deeply moved by Bobby's pitiful predicament. 'I couldn't bear to see how distressed, dispirited and constricted he looked,' he recalls. 'Poor Bobby was cooped up in this primitive, rundown cage with barely enough space in which to turn himself around.'

Peter's partner Rachael remembers his anguish only too well. 'He'd never seen an animal in such dire straits,' she says. 'He felt compelled to do something straight away for this poor lion. I saw how desperate he was to give Bobby a decent home. It was a reaction of human compassion.'

Peter first made his acquaintance with Bobby when the lion was just about existing – 'living' was almost too generous a word – at Broxbourne Zoo in Hertfordshire. At that time the zoo was widely regarded as the very worst in Britain and, despite Bobby's poor condition, the lion was its main attraction due simply to its rarity value.

The meeting between big cat and big-hearted man turned out to be momentous. It was to have life-changing consequences for both in a manner neither could have possibly foreseen. At the time, Yvonne Cullum was the only keeper who cared for Bobby and most of the animals. She had not been paid for many months by the previous owner, but when Peter purchased Broxbourne Zoo, he not only offered Yvonne a salary but he also backdated it. Yvonne was devoted and fully committed to Bobby and his welfare.

For Bobby, Peter's arrival was the start of a totally unexpected and desperately welcome upturn in his circumstances and the promise of a longer, cared-for life. For Peter it was a sudden, heartfelt calling that in time was to have a remarkable impact on the world's most endangered and rarest big cats and on the conservation of wildlife in general in many different countries around the world.

Broxbourne Zoo had just been placed on the market as part of an area of 24 acres of land up for sale in rural Hertfordshire. Peter candidly admits that his initial interest in the sale was not the zoo itself but the land on which it stood. In reality he was interested in it only as a potentially suitable site on which to park the large fleet of seventy coaches and buses he had assembled while becoming the leading independent passenger road transport company in the south-east of England.

For Peter, the existence of the zoo was incidental, but for him and all other would-be buyers, the site carried a strict condition of sale: the purchase of the land would include the zoo. That was enough to scare off several potential buyers, but not Peter Sampson. With the support of his family, he paid back over five years £100,000, which in today's valuation would be in excess of £2m, for the site and, again with their support and full agreement, he made it his first avowed priority to create for Bobby a home worthy of the name and to treat the lion with the respect he deserved. He would ensure Bobby had a comfortable life worth living till the end of his days.

Once he was given the go-ahead, Peter began work in earnest to build a spacious enclosure befitting a big cat. The project included constructing a proper house alongside the new enclosure in which the lion could sleep and shelter. Money was tight at the time for Peter, but nothing was going to hold him back. His enthusiasm for the task was infectious, and such was the loyalty of the staff of his transport business that employees, including drivers, fitters and welders from his workshops, and even office workers, willingly rallied round alongside family and friends of the Sampsons to help out, often giving up evenings, weekends and days off to the cause of rehoming Bobby.

Spurred on by this collective effort, Peter soon got the job done with the help of his inspired improvisation of the use of second-hand telegraph poles for fencing. Peter's own welding skills ensured the enclosure would be totally secure.

Finally, the day dawned for the rehoming of the lion. For Bobby's transfer Peter had constructed a special crate which could be carried in the style of a sedan chair. A team of four men positioned back and front lifted the crate on sturdy long poles and placed it on to a trailer attached to a tractor. With Peter at the wheel of the tractor, the trailer was towed into Bobby's new house alongside the specially built enclosure. It remained only for a connecting hatch to be raised to allow the lion the chance to venture out into his newly created compound.

There were shouts of encouragement to Bobby as his head first emerged, peering inquisitively through the hatch. The lion paused uncertainly for a moment to eye up his new surroundings, and then the shouts turned to triumphant cheers from Peter and other excited onlookers when, still looking understandably tentative and bemused, Bobby gingerly made his way out on to the grass at a very gentle trot.

It was a moment which Peter says will remain in his memory for ever. 'I can't overstate the pleasure it gave me to move that lion out of the prison which had been its home for all its life,' he says. 'It was an incredible sight watching Bobby padding around with his paws feeling grass underfoot for the first time in his life. At first, he didn't even know what grass was, but within an hour he had become acclimatised to his new home. I'll never forget seeing him run for the first time ever, and in freedom – not in total freedom, but in the best freedom we could give him.

'I can honestly say it was one of the happiest moments of my life. It stands out as a real highlight. It was also confirmation for me that we had made the right decision in buying the zoo. Giving Bobby a run on grass made us realise that this was what we now wanted to do. We were going to change our lifestyle from running a bus and coach company to looking after animals.'

Watching Bobby take those first steps on to grass remains the most heart-warming of memories for the entire Sampson family. 'Even now, forty years on, I can feel myself welling up at the thought of it,' says Peter's son Steve. 'Without doubt that was one of the best moments of owning Paradise Wildlife Park.'

Bobby the lion was being forced to lead a pathetic life until he was saved by Peter's instinctive desire to rescue him. Peter derived immense satisfaction from the sight of a revitalised Bobby exploring his spacious new enclosure with increasing confidence and a suddenly acquired zest for life, but he could never have imagined that this lion would be just the first of many hundreds, probably thousands, of big cats of various species in different, far-flung areas of the world on which he would have an impact in a variety of ways, most notably as founder of The Big Cat Sanctuary in Kent.

Bobby had a new life courtesy of Peter Sampson. Peter began a new life courtesy of Bobby.

CHAPTER TWO
War Baby

'I took an interest in the animals at the little farm at my school. That was way preferable to doing maths'
— *Peter Sampson*

Peter Charles Sampson could hardly have arrived in the world at a more critical time in history. He was born on 24 September 1939, exactly three weeks after Britain's Prime Minister Neville Chamberlain had made the grim official announcement to the nation on BBC radio that Britain was now at war with Germany. Peter took his first breath on a day when the stark reality of war was beginning to register in the minds of the British population. On that day, a Sunday, the first anti-submarine mines were being laid in the straits of Dover, and Germany's Luftwaffe were demonstrating in Poland what London could expect from the skies by bombing Warsaw for the first time and reducing entire streets to rubble.

It was relatively common for babies to be born at home at the time, and there was much rejoicing in the household of Gladys and Sidney Sampson when their baby son was safely delivered at the couple's tiny terraced cottage at Walton Road, Rye Park, Hoddesdon, in Hertfordshire. He was the couple's first and, as it was to transpire, only child.

Peter's Rye Park birthplace, a suburb of Hoddesdon, is situated some 20 miles (32 km) north of London in the Lea valley and, fittingly for Peter, it has a long and notable history as a coaching stop on the route from London to Cambridge. At its height during the 18th century, more than thirty-five horse-drawn coaches a day would pass through the town, and 200 years on, it would be Peter's own fleet of coaches and his company, Sampson Coaches and Travel, which would dominate the area in the field of transport.

Peter spent the earliest years of his life in the little Rye Park cottage where he was born. To say that the Sampson family home had its limitations is an understatement. 'Our house had no electricity, we had gas lamps for lighting downstairs, candles for lighting upstairs and a solitary water tap in the kitchen,' Peter recalls.

'There was no bathroom, but we had an old tin bath hanging outside on a nail on the back door. It was brought into the kitchen at the end of every week for Friday bath night. The bath was filled up with hot water with the help of a floor-standing gas water boiler and I was given a bath and then handed a clean vest and pants for me to wear the following day to last the next week.

'The loo was at the bottom of the garden, and my grandfather Charles Ison regularly came to the house at the weekend with a batch of newspapers, which he'd cut into squares and hang on a string for us to use as toilet paper.'

Life was simple in the extreme, but Peter has only fond memories of the house. 'It wasn't much,' he says, 'but when you're a kid you don't know any different, and you never miss what you don't have. For me, it was just home, but to this day I have no idea whether we owned the house or rented it.'

A sign of the tough times ahead for the Sampson family came when Peter was just three days old. As part of the War Budget, income tax was raised to its highest ever figure of seven shillings and sixpence in the pound (just over 37p in today's money). For a young couple with a baby, that represented a significant dent in the meagre income of Peter's father, working as a painter and decorator.

Just fifty days after Peter's birth, the first German bombs were dropped on English soil and, along with everyone else in Britain, Sid and Gladys must have wondered and worried over what lay in store for them and their infant son. It's impossible not to overstress how bleak the outlook was for the nation and for the Sampsons as they prepared for a wartime winter with their baby boy in 1939.

Peter was just three months old when there was further hardship for his parents to endure with the imposition of food rationing in Britain for the first time since 1918. The couple had Peter's extra mouth to feed and the rigid rationing laws demanded the compulsory registration of every household with their local shops. Everyone was required to have an ID and a medical card, including young Peter. 'So there was not much food about,' he says. 'No eggs, no bananas, sugar, coffee, butter, cheese – the list was endless.'

A saving grace for Sid and Gladys was the fact that several family members lived close by. Gladys had four sisters and two brothers all living locally. Naturally they all doted on the new addition to the family and rallied round to offer help, food and babysitting whenever needed. Peter's grandfather Charles, Gladys's father, also lived in nearby Rye Road. He owned and ran a bicycle shop and repair service and he also had a sizeable garden with a large garage and a workshop where he carried out car repairs. He was one of only fourteen people in Hoddesdon town who owned a car at that time. The workshop is still rented to this day to Peter's godson, David King, although it was sold many years ago.

The proximity of so many members of the Sampson kin was a comfort to them all, especially when the menfolk were called up and dutifully went off to war. Peter was still less than a year old when his father received his military call-up papers. Within days Gladys waved Sid off to do his duty for king and country. Like every wife left behind to keep the home fires burning, Gladys must have had doubts as to whether her husband would ever see her and his son again.

Peter's own recollections of the later years of the war are inevitably sketchy at best as he was so young. As a baby, he would not have registered that his father somehow managed to send home a card for him in time for his first birthday. And he was four months short of his sixth birthday by the time his dad came home just as the country was celebrating Victory in Europe Day.

One clear memory of the war years for Peter was the presence of girls from the Women's Land Army who arrived at the house to stay as lodgers with his mother. Land Girls, as they were called, were women who volunteered to help with the war effort by taking on a variety of jobs in agriculture ranging from milking cows to general farm work, from cutting down trees to working in saw mills, driving tractors and even rat-catching. Conspicuous in their green jerseys, brown breeches and brown felt slouch hats, they became a familiar sight for Peter around Hoddesdon by the time he was blowing out the five candles on his birthday cake in September 1944.

With Sid still away on military duty, Gladys patriotically opened up her home to provide accommodation for several Land Girls. 'At one point we had three of them staying with us all at the same time,' Peter recalls. 'I have no idea how we managed to have them all stay in our tiny home. But somehow we all crammed in.' Inevitably, these girls of the 'forgotten Army', as they came to be labelled, were quick to make a fuss of the bright, sandy-haired little boy who lived with his mum in Walton Road. Peter by now had started school at Walton Primary, a short walk away in the same road.

For young lads growing up in Britain in the late 1940s and 1950s, life was very different from what it is today. Pre-school days were spent in a manner that would be considered desperately dull nowadays. Television was in its infancy and very few people could afford television sets anyway. Wind-up gramophones and 78 rpm records were something parents could buy only as a luxury, and as money was scarce, there was no commercial teenage culture.

As the Sampsons had no electricity at their cottage, entertainment at home centred on the family wireless set which was powered by a battery accumulator. This required regular recharging at the local shop, which provided a temporary replacement on loan for the price of sixpence while the original one was recharging.

For Gladys, it was a huge relief to have her husband home safe and well after military service, which had included a long posting to Burma. But for Peter, bonding with his father was far from easy. For the first five years of his life he had not seen him. Now father and son had to get to know each other, and Peter admits that for years his dad remained little more than a stranger to him.

The end of the war may have brought peace but not prosperity for the country. Times were hard for everyone and the Sampsons found life in post-war Britain to be exceedingly tough. It was not until Peter had reached the age of thirteen that strict rationing of food, clothes and petrol was lifted.

As with millions of men who had been called up, Sidney Sampson found returning home after the war required considerable readjustment to domestic life. Jobs and housing were scarce but, modest though his house was, Sid at least had a home to come back to and, importantly, he had a small son to get to know and raise.

To put food on the table for his family Sidney set up his own painting and decorating business. He had never held a driving licence and could never afford to own a car, so of necessity he largely worked locally. According to workmates, Sidney was a hard-working man who always kept his word and wasn't interested in small handyman jobs because he thought big – all characteristics which people came to recognise in Peter when he went into business.

Not long after Sidney's return from the war his mother died, and Peter found himself in new surroundings when his dad decided to move his family to live with his widowed father six miles away at his Hertfordshire house in Clarendon Road, Cheshunt. These new living arrangements took some getting used to for Peter. As travel had been so difficult during the war years, he had rarely seen his grandfather and thus had precious little time to get to know him. All he knew of him was that he worked in a factory in north London and that he was a piano tuner by trade. Once Peter had settled in, his grandfather offered to teach him to play the piano. 'But for some strange reason, I wasn't interested at the time,' he says. 'It's one of my greatest regrets that I passed up that opportunity.' Sadly, his grandfather died a few months later.

Moving home meant Peter becoming a pupil at the British School, an old Victorian establishment in College Road, Cheshunt. But he was there for only three terms before being moved to another school, Burleigh Primary, again just a short walk away in Blind Man's Lane, Cheshunt. It had the distinction of being the first new school in the country to open since the war. Many years later both Peter's son Steve and daughter Lynn attended Burleigh Primary School.

In the holidays and at weekends Peter often travelled by bus to visit family in Rye Park, where he spent much of his time with his cousins Terry Keates and Barry Oakman, who were two years younger than Peter. Terry and Barry were also from one-child families and the boys grew up almost as brothers.

Peter's parents quickly adapted to their new surroundings in Cheshunt and soon built up a network of new friends they met up with at their local pub, The Old English Gentleman. Pubs were hubs of entertainment for millions of people in towns and villages right across the country after the war and The Old English Gentleman was no exception, with music nights and teams competing in traditional pub games of darts, dominoes and shove ha'penny. Pub regulars occasionally went off on a coach trip to Southend, and many years later they would depart as passengers on one of Peter's coaches.

Peter remembers many a time he was left sitting outside the pub with a packet of crisps while his dad enjoyed a few bevvies inside. 'My parents would be at The Old English Gentleman most evenings,' he recalls, 'and there would be times when they'd return home after closing time a bit worse for wear, bringing with them a few friends and a few bottles. I can remember evenings when I'd be upstairs in my bedroom, lying under the bedclothes trying to sleep, and I'd hear them enjoying themselves downstairs. By then they had a radiogram and it had the loudest bass tone you've ever heard. The music would be going full blast throughout the house late into the night. If I had a glass of water by my bed, I'd see the water vibrating in the glass.'

Peter joined the Cubs and, as he got older, he enrolled with the 1st Cheshunt Boy Scouts, which gave him a good grounding and the opportunity to go away on camping experiences.

Life was largely routine for Peter, with a joint for lunch on a Sunday, cold meat on a Monday, and mince on the Tuesday. Outings with his mother were limited by her insistence she would never travel on the London Underground, never get into a lift, never ride an escalator, and she refused to fly.

The big treat for Peter was his grandfather driving the family up to High Beech to have a picnic. When family finances allowed in the school summer holidays, Peter travelled by train from Broxbourne with his parents or with his cousin Terry and his parents to Clacton or Great Yarmouth to stay in bed and breakfast guest houses.

When Peter was nine years old his grandfather drove him up to London with a group of family members to see a show at the Finsbury Park Empire, at that time second only to the London Palladium as the capital's number one theatre. Peter cannot recall much of the show itself, probably a pantomime, but he remembers its very strange ending. As the applause died down at the final curtain, police came into the building and took to the stage to inform the audience that the fog outside was so dense that it was unsafe to venture out of the building.

Back then on dark winter nights, London was liable to be enveloped by a thick smog, known as a 'pea souper' because of its yellow-brownish colour, due to air pollution from chimney soot and poisonous sulphur dioxide. The police warning to Peter in the packed audience at the Finsbury Park Empire that night was no idle caution. There had been occasions in London when visibility was almost nil and there were reports of people falling into the Thames and drowning because they could not see the river right in front of them.

On this occasion the police advised the theatre audience that for their own safety they should remain in the theatre throughout the night and make no effort to head for home until it was light in the morning. Peter, his relatives and his grandad and a 2,200-strong audience duly spent an uncomfortable night trying to get some shuteye in the theatre seats they had already been occupying for three hours. Years later Peter found himself driving home from north London through a pea souper by following closely behind a bus which in turn was following a man walking in front of it holding a flare.

***

Peter was still a young schoolboy when he first showed an interest in breeding animals, the first hint of a passion which unbeknown to him at the time was later to dominate his life. As well as keeping chickens in pens in the garden, he began to breed white satin rabbits, a rare species noted for their smooth coats. His interest was sparked while he was on a bicycle ride through Enfield during which he learned of a prize-winning breeder living close by. 'He showed me his rabbits and all the rosettes he had won for breeding,' Peter recalls. 'So I decided to get a couple of rabbits for myself and I ended up entering them for competitions and shows and beating him to the top prizes.

'One of the most exciting things for me as a boy was opening the rabbit hutch one morning and seeing the first baby rabbits I'd bred. As they started to grow they were the prettiest things I'd ever seen.' The satisfaction and excitement Peter felt at the arrival of baby animals was something which would be repeated over and over in years to come at The Big Cat Sanctuary and at Paradise Wildlife Park.

Peter built his own rabbit hutches, and he became such a successful breeder of white satins that he regularly won first prize at local rabbit shows. His chief interest aside from the rabbits was sport, with football, and particularly speedway, to the fore, thanks to his uncle Steve Ison, his mother's brother, who was showing such promise as a rider from his training days at the local Rye House speedway track near his home.

Steve was just starting to register regular team points for Harringay in speedway's prestigious National League Division One when disaster struck and his life was cut tragically short. He met an untimely death while travelling with several other riders on road bikes on their way to a speedway meeting at Rayleigh, Essex. Steve was involved in a three-vehicle crash near Romford on the London to Southend road and he was killed outright. The chilling irony that Steve had died on a road motorcycle on a public highway, after risking life and limb in speedway, was not lost on family, relatives, friends, team mates and colleagues.

Steve Ison died on 25 September 1948, just one day after Peter's ninth birthday. 'His death hit me terribly hard,' Peter remembers. 'That was the first big setback of my life. It was a horrible shock and desperately hard for me to take in at my young age. I idolised Steve and suddenly he wasn't there anymore. He was dead at the young age of twenty-six. For anyone to lose their life so young is terribly sad, but it also meant that Steve never got the chance to fulfil his great potential.'

It was a shattering blow for the Ison, Sampson, Keates and Oakman relatives and no less for Peter. Such was the respect and general affection for the young rider that a huge crowd of mourners gathered at St Cuthbert's church at Whitley Road, Rye Park, for Steve's funeral. It turned out to be the largest attendance for a funeral that Hoddesdon locals could ever remember.

Steve Ison's death occurred more than seventy-five years ago, but Peter has never forgotten his uncle and vows he never will. He named his own son Steve after his uncle, and Steve Ison's name still occasionally crops up with much fondness in Peter's conversation. It was recently drawn to Peter's attention that Steve's gravestone at the cemetery in Ware Road, Hoddesdon, was crumbling and in need of attention, and it was Peter who quietly took it upon himself to check up on it and organise payment for repairs and restoration.

As we will see, Steve Ison had a huge impact on Peter's life and the link with his uncle lived on when one of Steve's closest friends, Scotty Weekes, came to work with Peter many years later in his coach and travel business.

By the time he was eleven, Peter had moved school once again, to an old Victorian establishment called Gews Corner at Cheshunt. But he was a pupil there for just three terms before moving once more to yet another new school, Riversmead Secondary Modern in Cheshunt.

In the year below him was a boy by the name of Harry Webb, who in a few years would become the singer with a local music combo called Dick Teague's Skiffle Group before eventually changing his name and finding worldwide fame as Cliff Richard. As they were in different forms, Peter's and Harry's lives rarely crossed at school but Peter recalls playing table tennis with the singer at a local boys' club and seeing his early performances at local events and parties.

When Peter was thirteen, he suffered a major setback in his young life. Along with two other local boys, he developed rheumatic fever, a disease which can affect the heart, joints, brain and skin, and he suffered badly enough to wind up spending eight weeks in Hertford hospital and nine months off school.

It was a devastating blow for Peter just at a time when he was growing fast, and it left him with a heart murmur and other problems which warranted the nine long months recovering at home. 'How I caught rheumatic fever was a bit of a mystery,' he says. 'I don't know for certain, but myself and the other two boys put it down to playing football in the local park, where we used to have a drink from the brook nearby.'

Nine months off school seemed like an eternity for a boy who had just entered his teens and was normally full of energy and had developed a passion for playing football and other sports. Now he was under strict orders to rest up, recuperate and recover his strength quietly at home. His illness meant he was unable to take any part in school sports for twelve months. During his recuperation Peter missed his schoolfriends desperately and longed for the day he could kick a football around with them again. Inevitably his school education suffered. In the classroom he was now almost a year behind pupils the same age.

'When I was finally fit enough to return to school, I had a difficult time catching up because everyone tried to wrap me up in cotton wool,' he explains. 'Everyone kept telling me I had to be so careful about everything I did and that I must look after myself. They all tried to treat me with kid gloves.

'My confidence wasn't good at the best of times in those days, but now it was shot. It hit me harder than I realised then. Already I wasn't the brightest kid on the block, and now I was missing lessons too.'

Gradually Peter was allowed to ease himself back into school and resume living a normal life. 'It wasn't easy trying to catch up in the classroom with everybody else well ahead. To offset that, I played every sport I could. I became greatly involved in football, rugby, cricket and swimming. It was far better than attending lessons, although I realise now that was not the brightest idea. I even joined the gardening club and volunteered to work in the pets corner. This was a little farm at the school with a few animals and I took an interest in that as it was way preferable to doing maths.'

Then, just when he seemed to be getting over all of his problems, life dealt Peter another shattering blow. His father committed suicide.

Peter was lying in bed one morning when the unmistakeable smell of gas filtered upstairs into his bedroom. He immediately ran downstairs to be greeted by the distressing sight of his dad lying on the floor with his head in the gas oven. 'He was already dead and had turned blue,' Peter recalls. 'I remember turning off the gas, calling my mum to come downstairs and then the ambulance and police arriving.

'I was fourteen at the time and it was a terrible shock. I was sent away to stay with my cousin Terry for a month at Rye Park. When I returned home, the thing that seemed so strange to me was that I found we were still cooking our dinner in the same gas oven.'

It's not difficult to imagine the devastating effect this tragic event had on Peter. But he says: 'My first thoughts were that my dad had let both me and my mum down. I felt some anger that we were now carrying his debts and his problems and now that he wasn't around I'd have to be the one to sort them out. A determination to sort things out is something I've since carried with me all my life.'

In later years in his maturity, Peter came to regard his father's suicide differently and with more understanding: 'It may have been down to drinking, or spending more than he was earning, financial trouble. But it could also have been down to stress from the war. Why he took his own life I just don't know for sure, but I swore that I would never do to my family what my dad had done to me. No matter how bad things might ever be, I swore it would never happen.

'Sadly, I feel I never really got to know my father at all. I didn't get to see him until I was six because he was away in the war, and I was fourteen when he died. He never really became involved in my life as those were years when I was at school and he was out working.

'My dad's death also set me back even further at school. I was kept away from the classroom for a month until the funeral had been held and life had got back to some sort of normality. Of course the news of my dad's suicide had got around the school very quickly, and when I went back I found myself receiving unwanted attention. Other pupils would be talking about it among themselves, whispering and pointing at me in the playground.

'I didn't do at all well at school and part of the reason was that I lacked confidence. I think being an only child doesn't do you any favours in life. My father had died, I didn't have any brothers and sisters to bounce off, and I was quite shy.'

Traumatic as it was at the time, there are many close to Peter who believe that his father's death in the most terrible circumstances had the effect of spurring Peter into resolving he would never waste his own life; he would make the most of himself and give it his best shot in whatever he chose to do. Friends also believe that his father's suicide taught Peter that the most important thing in life is life itself, and not just human life. Peter's subsequent tireless determination to protect and conserve big cats and other rare animal species threatened with extinction, and to generate new life as a breeder, is testament to that. 'Sadly, animals don't live forever. Death is inevitable, but it always upsets me when one of our cats dies,' he says.

The immediate practical upshot of the tragedy in the Sampson household was that Peter's mother had no option but to go out to work to make ends meet. Gladys found herself a job working in the kitchens at the Woolworths store at Waltham Cross and she also began taking in lodgers. For his part, Peter took on both morning and evening paper rounds seven days a week. To help his mother pay the bills, he also took on a full day's work on Saturdays with a butcher's round at the local Co-op.

'I became the butcher's delivery boy, riding an old-fashioned tradesman's bike with a large basket on the front. The meat would get wrapped up and labelled and I'd set off and cycle up to 12 miles a day delivering to homes in a five-mile radius. I'd be out delivering in wind and rain, all weathers, and occasionally the rain would wash the writing off the labels and make the names and addresses unreadable. I'm sure there were a few people who got the wrong delivery from what they'd ordered.

'It was a typical butcher's shop with sawdust on the floor and wooden benches and blocks that I was required to scrub. It was a good grounding for me in that I had to work long and hard, and at the end of the day the shop manager was good enough to wrap up a few sausages for me to take home.

'I eat very little meat these days, but that butcher's job has left me with a strong dislike of chicken. As Christmas neared, there would be lots of chickens brought into the butcher's and to keep them moist and tender they were dipped in brine. The smell was terrible. Ever since then I've been unable to eat chicken.'

Despite the deaths of his grandad Charles Ison and, a few months later, his grandmother Eliza Ison, things were looking up financially for Peter and his mother and, as he prepared to leave school at fifteen, he could reflect on a boyhood that had certainly been eventful on a personal level. He had come through the war years, attended five different schools but missed months of school time, and most of his family had died – his father by suicide, his favourite uncle in a road crash, and all four of his grandparents. He wondered what the rest of his life had in store.

CHAPTER THREE
The Apprentice

'Other young lads could buy smart clothes and take a girl out. I couldn't even afford a new tyre for my bike'
— *Peter Sampson*

Peter was fifteen when he left Riversmead school. 'I should have been sad to leave,' he reflects. 'I should have enjoyed my schooldays. But the day I left was one of the happiest days of my life at that point. I came to know that should not have been the case.'

Having missed so many lessons in the classroom due to rheumatic fever, Peter left Riversmead with no academic qualifications. He was unsure where his life was going other than hopefully securing a job as a motorbike mechanic with Harry White's motorcycle shop, located in College Road almost opposite his school. Harry White regularly took on one apprentice every year and that was the job many of Peter's fellow school leavers coveted. Peter was no exception, but he says: 'I lacked confidence and was quite shy. So I stood at the back of the queue and didn't even get an interview for the job.'

Close friends Allen Richardson and John Medcalf also left Riversmead at the same time as Peter, and all three applied for apprenticeships in the motor trade with Haslemere Garage at Waltham Abbey. It was by far the largest of its kind in the area, employing more than sixty fitters and paint sprayers in several big workshops. To their collective relief and joy, all three school pals were taken on as apprentices at the garage with a starting wage of two pounds ten shillings (£2.50) a week.

Every morning the three teenagers set off on their bicycles together in all weathers to pedal the five miles to the garage ready to start work at 7.45 a.m. Peter and Allen were assigned to the car workshops and John to the commercial workshops. Finishing time was 6 p.m., which made for a long day, but in Peter's case it was occasionally made all the longer by the unpleasant attitude of the fitter allocated to show him the ropes and train him up. For some unfathomable reason he took an instant dislike to Peter which regularly manifested itself just when it was close to knocking-off time.

At 5.30 towards the end of each working day, the fitters called for the apprentices to carry out various clean-up duties. They were required to sweep out the pits underneath the cars they had been working on, then lay down a clean bed of sawdust before carefully cleaning every spanner and any other tools they had been using, before returning the tools to the workboxes. They would then be ready to knock off at 6 p.m. However, the fitter allocated to Peter developed a malicious habit of waiting until 5.50 p.m. and then somehow managing to find just the tiniest trace of grease still remaining on one of the spanners. Spitefully he took great delight in emptying the entire box of tools back down into the pit, forcing Peter to stay behind to clean the whole lot all over again.

Peter has not forgotten him. 'I was fifteen, just a kid really. He was much older than me and a nasty piece of work. Whatever I did was wrong in his eyes. Everybody was ready to knock off at six o'clock to go home, everybody except me. I'd be back down the pit cleaning spanners and unable to get away till way past six. Mind you, ever since then I clean every spanner I use as if it was a knife or fork.'

This bully-boy behaviour towards Peter resulted in his first year at Haslemere Garage proving to be far from easy, not helped by an unfortunate but avoidable accident involving the Haslemere Garage boiler. In winter months apprentices were required to take it in turns to clear out and refill with coke the furnace which heated up the boiler. A can of paraffin was on hand to help the furnace to fire up, but on one occasion when it was Peter's turn, unbeknown to him, the can had mistakenly been filled with petrol. When he lit the fire, the top of the boiler blew off, burning his hair, singeing off his eyebrows and landing him in Moorfields Eye Hospital for two days. He suffered eye damage which has hindered his sight to this day.

The mechanic's nasty behaviour continued until it came to the attention of the workshop foreman, an experienced and skilled mechanic with a kindly nature and a wise head on his shoulders. He noticed the unpleasant animosity his young apprentice was being forced to endure and stepped in. He had observed that, despite the hostile work atmosphere, Peter had always shown himself to be a willing, diligent, hard worker and a quick learner and as such could now be trusted to work on vehicles on his own. Changing wheels and brakes and generally servicing cars away from his tormentor came as a welcome relief for the teenager. 'I could start to work on the cars on my own overseen by the foreman,' Peter says. 'That felt very special.'

Peter earned just £2 10s (£2.50) a week as an apprentice, and by the time he had given his mother £2 for his keep, he was left with just ten shillings (50p) in his pocket. There were essentially just two options for a Saturday night out for Peter to consider. It was either a dance night at the Tudor Hall or an outing to the cinema with his friends John and Allen. The cinema proved the favourite option for teenagers like Peter although it meant taking a bus to Waltham Cross and then facing a tricky choice. They could either catch the bus back home or pay for a plate of beans on toast and a mug of tea at a small café and then walk home. It's hard to believe now, but either way, he could find himself still with change in his pocket from a ten-shilling note (50p) at the end of the night. 'With inflation over the years, people can earn more in one hour than I did in one month,' he says.

Now with a regular job and a steady, if meagre, income, Peter and his mother Gladys were just getting out of the financial troubles left behind by Peter's father when she unexpectedly decided to marry again. 'That was a big disappointment to me,' Peter says. 'She married a funny little man from

Liverpool called Ben Wheatley who had been a lodger at our house and was known to be a big drinker at the local pub. My mother was a nice-looking lady, so I couldn't understand why she'd chosen this particular man to marry. He was not my cup of tea. He was a chain-smoker and an alcoholic.

'Suddenly having a new stepfather was quite a change in my life. Since my father's death it had been just Mum and me, the two Sampsons, and now she wasn't Mrs. Sampson any more. Suddenly she was Mrs Wheatley and I was the last Sampson standing. That felt very strange to me.'

Peter was two-thirds of the way through his apprenticeship at the time and was making good progress at Haslemere Garage. But his wages had increased only minimally from the day he was hired and he started looking for more lucrative employment. He was growing up, eager to spread his wings, and for that he needed more money in his pocket.

Despite Peter's difficult relationship with his mother's new husband, it was Ben Wheatley who helped Peter find a job with much improved wages. Wheatley was working on a building site and managed to secure work for Peter alongside him at £7 10s (£7.50) a week, a significant increase on his take-home pay at Haslemere Garage.

The work mainly entailed fitting asbestos fire curtains into the roofs of large industrial buildings on the outskirts of London. At times it was perilous work carried out on special scaffolding towers on wheels, and more than once a dumper truck carelessly nudged the tower off kilter, leaving Peter momentarily hanging precariously from the roof like a trapeze artist.

Peter hated the work and the commuting. It often required a train journey from Cheshunt into London, then crossing London to catch another train out to factories and warehouses in the outer reaches of Kent. Other days found him catching a bus to Potters Bar, then walking three miles to catch another bus to Luton.

Peter has some regrets that he never completed his apprenticeship at Haslemere Garage. But, for a seventeen-year-old boy still living at home and growing up fast, a job offering more than twice the money in his pay packet at the end of each week was just too good to turn down. 'I knew I was never going to earn enough working at the garage,' he says. 'Other young working lads my age could afford to take a girl out and buy smart clothes whereas I couldn't afford even a new tyre for my bicycle.'

* * *

Throughout his teenage years Peter proved to be an enthusiastic and talented sportsman, representing Cheshunt Boys and Athletics Club at football, cricket, table tennis, swimming and gymnastics. But the pressing reason he wanted to earn more was because he had developed a serious ambition to be a speedway rider like his late uncle Steve Ison. The extra wages were especially welcome because he was carefully saving up enough money to buy his own speedway bike.

Once he had reached the age whereby he was old enough to ride a motorbike on the public highway, Peter bought himself an old Norton road bike which he learned to ride by setting off on regular trips to Hoddesdon to visit his grandfather. It was a far from ideal introduction to motorcycling. Peter could afford neither a helmet nor leathers, so he wore a bus driver's overcoat courtesy of two uncles who regularly drove buses on the Green Line routes. He also quickly discovered the limitations of the second-hand Norton he had purchased. After stopping in Hoddesdon he regularly found he was unable to get the bike started again. He could never work out whether it was an issue with the coil or a problem with the ignition. 'All I know is that more often than not I had to leave my bike at my grandfather's house and take the bus home.'

As soon as he felt he was proficient enough as a rider, Peter booked himself a motorcycle road test. But when the day came for the test, he had already sold his bike to help pay for a van. With a little help from his mother, Peter had traded in his bike for an old Fordson light commercial van which he had bought for £50. After taxing and insuring the Fordson, he swotted up on the Highway Code for two days, then chanced his luck by taking the van instead of a motorbike to the test centre in Hertford. 'When I explained to the examiner that I no longer owned a motorbike, I asked to be tested in the van,' Peter recounts. 'Amazingly he agreed. I know for a fact that would never happen in this day and age.

'I sailed through the Highway Code section of the test with flying colours. But when it came to me getting behind the wheel of the van, the examiner was surprised to find there was no passenger seat, just a box to sit on, and that the side window wouldn't open properly until I managed to rattle it down. He was also amazed to find that I drove my van with my left knee pressed against the gear lever. I had to explain that it was the only way to prevent it from jumping out of gear. I have to count my lucky stars because despite these hiccups I passed the test.'

* * *

After a year of working on the building sites, Peter spotted an advertisement in Cheshunt for a lorry and van driver required by Symonds, an engineering firm. Now that he possessed a driving licence and was capable of driving his own van, it was enough for Peter to find himself hired straight away despite having no experience of driving lorries. 'It was the start of a new life. My mum was still working but my wages had gone up to £10 a week and it was an interesting job in many ways, as I was driving down into Kent, all round London, and the Home Counties basically with a map in one hand and the steering wheel in the other.'

Initially Peter's lack of experience was shown up when his new job at Symonds got off to a humiliating start. 'I was asked to take their lorry out and I pulled across the high street before realising that I had no idea how to put it into reverse. To my embarrassment I had to leave the lorry stuck where it was while I went back to ask another driver: "Where's the reverse gear?"'

It was at Symonds where Peter met Johnny Arthur, a welder who was to become one of Peter's most treasured and lifelong friends. Known to everyone in Peter's circle as 'John the Welder', Johnny was several years older than Peter and he took him under his wing. They shared in common a passionate interest in motorbikes and speedway and as their friendship broadened they became almost like brothers. 'Meeting Johnny was one of the greatest good fortunes of my young life,' Peter acknowledges. 'Johnny was the king of welders and he taught me everything he knew about what was then gas welding and braising. He taught me all the skills and I will always be grateful to him for that.'

At work Johnny proved to be not just a mentor but a prankster. 'He would write little notes pretending they were from me, then place them on the work benches of the girls, asking them out on a date. It was very embarrassing for me because I was too shy to do anything about them. All I did was just blush.'

* * *

Peter may have lacked self-assurance in his teens but in a bid to meet and impress the girls he began taking ballroom dancing lessons at a dance school in Cheshunt. Together with his great pal Allen 'Mo' Richardson, Peter enrolled for lessons at the Dave Jones School of Dancing. Both figured the pathway to meeting girls would be a good deal smoother if they knew how to put one foot in front of the other in time to a musical beat.

At the dance school they were taught the waltz, the quickstep and the foxtrot as well as the rudiments of jiving. Now that rock 'n' roll was becoming the new ballroom fad thanks to the sudden popularity of Bill Haley and Elvis Presley, it was important to Peter and Mo to show that they were 'hep-cats' who were 'hip to the beat', as the trendy jargon had it at the time. The last thing they wanted was to be regarded as 'square' when they hit the dance floor.

Learning to jive as well as the basics of traditional ballroom dancing meant Peter and Mo had the chance to show off their nifty moves when they got up to dance at parties to the beat of Dick Teague's Skiffle Group, a fledgling local would-be rock 'n' roll band.

This combo was somewhat amateurish and lacked decent musical equipment at the time, but the group were enthusiastic enough to play occasionally at the Rye House pub and at the Rye House speedway clubroom. The word around the area was that the singer with Dick Teague's outfit, local lad Harry Webb, who, as we have seen, was at school with Peter, did a pretty good impression of his idol Elvis Presley when he stepped up to the microphone with his hair greased back, his top lip curled to try and look mean and his hips swinging like Elvis the pelvis. It nevertheless still came as a big surprise to the local community when Harry Webb became Cliff Richard and suddenly rose to stardom overnight.

Mo and Peter took their dancing lessons seriously enough, although neither found them easy, and they had no great expectations when it came to take their dance exams at the end of their course. On the day of the assessments Peter found to his dismay that he would be put through his paces not by one of the female instructors as his partner but by Dave Jones himself. 'I'd taken lessons to meet girls, and now I found myself dancing with a man in his seventies with a gammy leg,' was Peter's bemused reaction. 'I asked Dave how he rated my chances and he replied: "Just don't fall over." Happily I didn't, and nor did Mo, and we both ended up passing with a bronze rating, but sadly not a gold.' The bronze award did, however, go some way to Peter overcoming his shyness in asking a girl to dance in case she might decline. In later years Peter's children went to the Dave Jones School of Dancing and won gold awards.

***

Although he was yet to achieve his ambition of becoming a speedway rider, Peter was by now very much a part of the Rye House speedway fraternity. He was mingling with motorbike enthusiasts, fellow speedway fans, mechanics, pit crews and riders, many of them considerably older than himself. He forged firm friendships with several riders, including Mike 'Broady' Broadbank, Brian Brett, Colin Pratt and Gerry King, and in the spring of 1959 Peter was thrilled to be asked to become godfather to David King, the son of Gerry and his wife Freda.

At weekends Peter would regularly pack up some sandwiches and follow riders to speedway tracks around the country to support them. Later that summer of 1959 he travelled with Gerry to help him out in the pits while Gerry raced for the Swindon speedway team. It did not end well, Peter recalls. 'Sadly, Gerry crashed heavily on the top bend of the Swindon track and the rider coming up behind him was unable to avoid Gerry and crashed into him. He sustained life-threatening injuries and spent many weeks recovering in hospital. Although I was in a state of shock, I had to load up Gerry's bike into his van and drive it back home through the night. On arrival I was still in such a state of shock that I couldn't remember how I'd made it home.' Gerry's injuries were so severe that he never rode speedway again. Peter remains good friends with him to this day.

'Broady' Broadbank was another rider who became a very special friend. Like Peter's late uncle Steve Ison, Broady had first been discovered as a rider at the Rye House track. They became such good buddies that during the 1955 speedway season when Broady was riding for Rye House, Peter arranged for him to move in with him and his mother at the Cheshunt family home in Clarendon Road. Peter was then sixteen, and he looked up to Broady, who was seven years older almost to the day, with such respect that he generously volunteered to move into the box room at the top of the house to allow just-married Broady and his new wife to occupy the large double bedroom at the rear of the house.

'I wasn't bothered about moving into the box room,' Peter says. 'It was worth it just to have Broady around at home to talk to and learn about all things speedway. That was a massive bonus. He was my boyhood idol and, for me, it was like having the king coming to stay. At the end of the speedway season, Broady asked me if I could get him work alongside me on the building sites and I did manage to get him a job. We'd arrive for work together in the bright red Triumph TR7 sports car Broady had bought with his earnings as a top speedway rider. I can still see the heads turning when we showed up for work in that special car.'

The ability and courage Broady had shown as a Rye House rider soon earned him a contract in 1956 to ride for the Wembley Lions, which subsequently necessitated his having to move out of Peter's Clarendon Road home. But that was not the only change in Peter's home life. His mother's marriage had been difficult and it failed to last. One day Wheatley simply disappeared, apparently back to Liverpool. 'My stepfather did a vanishing act and I never saw him again' is Peter's stark recollection.

While his good friend Broady was taking a step up into speedway's top division with the Wembley Lions, Peter was taking his first steps towards becoming a speedway rider himself. On a trip to Wembley with Broady, Peter was able to purchase his own speedbike. With his savings and a little help from Broady he bought a bike from former Wembley Lions rider Jeff Lloyd for £60. That in itself was a thrill for Peter because Jeff was a top international rider who qualified for the Speedway World Championship finals three times.

The purchase of Jeff's bike was to give Peter an introduction to an exciting new chapter in his young life – riding very fast around speedway tracks on two wheels. And without brakes.

Armed with a newfound confidence gained from owning his own speedway bike and from knowing that he could perform some adequate footwork on the dance floor, Peter plucked up courage to arrange a first date with a pretty local girl called Carol, who had been a contemporary at school with Peter and was friendly with Cliff Richard's sisters.

Peter had got to know Carol through her brother and her father, who both shared a similar interest in motorbikes. But no sooner had Peter asked her out than his great pal Johnny Arthur chose to intervene. Knowing Peter's burgeoning desire to become a speedway rider, Johnny had some advice for the teenager. 'Do you seriously want to become a speedway rider?' he asked. 'Because if you do, you need to devote time to it. You don't want to be spending your time going out with girls.'

Johnny, wiser and more experienced in the ways of the world, could be very persuasive, as Peter recalls: 'He was ten years older than me, and he'd become something of a father figure. So I did as I was told and I didn't turn up for the date.' Happily for Peter and Carol, they have long since been able to laugh about the night he stood her up. She forgave him and they remained good friends.

CHAPTER FOUR

On Track

'Suddenly I saw another rider overtaking me while casually puffing away on a cigarette'

— *Peter Sampson*

As with many young boys growing up in the 1950s and 1960s, Peter Sampson was first drawn to the sport of speedway by the thrilling spectacle of daring young men racing around a black cinder track astride powerful motorbikes – without any brakes.

But, as we have learned, for Peter the special attraction of speedway had been the chance to watch his favourite rider in action, his uncle Steve Ison. He had been one of the sport's brightest young stars until his untimely death.

Young Peter had worshipped Steve, and it was always a thrilling experience for him to watch his uncle scorching around the local Rye House track and to bask in reflected glory whenever Steve won points for his team. Born a stone's throw from the track, Steve had been a much admired young rider who seemed destined for major success within the sport until his life was so cruelly cut short. 'Steve was already in his twenties and training to be a speedway rider when I was just five,' Peter fondly recalls. 'When speedway took off after the war years, he'd managed to progress into the Harringay team, and he'd become the hero I looked up to along with my cousin Terry.'

In common with millions of fans around the world who followed the sport in its golden post-war era, Peter had nothing but admiration and respect for the courage and skill of the riders as they diced with danger on the track. He was awed by their expertise as they jostled for superiority and position while struggling to control the sliding back wheels of their speedway bikes when they accelerated into the bends.

While his uncle Steve was becoming a star rider on the track at nearby Rye House, it was inevitable Peter would take a keen interest while growing up. He was thrilled by the whole atmosphere of speedway from his very first visit as a young boy. There was always a buzz of anticipation running through the crowd as the riders came on to the track and lined up awaiting the sound of the klaxon indicating two minutes to the start. Racing away as soon as the tapes went up, the riders would be roared on by an excited crowd whose cheering strained to be heard above the throaty growl of the speedway bike engines.

Speedway meetings never failed to excite youngsters like Peter. He came to enjoy the whole experience: the colour, the heady mix in the air of oil and dust, the smell in the nostrils of Castrol R engine oil and the fumes of methanol fuel from the exhausts of the bikes racing around the oval track. And there was always that hint of danger in the air.

It takes guts and nerves of steel to be a speedway rider. Peter knew that as well as having no brakes, speedway machines had just a solitary gear, a clutch, and a 500cc engine with the ability to accelerate from 0 to 60 mph in under 2.5 seconds. That, as riders and fans were quick to point out, was faster than a Formula One racing car back in the day.

In Peter's youth this spectacular action on two wheels enjoyed such wide appeal that speedway could draw a crowd of as many as 85,000 fans to the track at Wembley to watch their helmeted heroes in action. A London Cup match between Wembley and West Ham once drew not only the capacity crowd of 85,000 but a further ticketless 20,000 fans, who were locked outside listening to a BBC radio commentary on the action via loudspeakers set up in the car park. That's how fanatical supporters were.

Speedway stars of yesteryear were as famous as footballers today. In 1966 the world speedway champion, New Zealander Barry Briggs, was voted third in the BBC Sports Personality of the Year poll. It was a measure of his and the sport's popularity and his standing as a sportsman that he was only beaten to the cherished BBC sports trophy by two of England's World Cup-winning football heroes, Bobby Moore and Geoff Hurst.

Unlike today's soccer idols, speedway stars were invariably accessible to fans after race meetings. Most were only too happy to stay behind after their rides to sign autographs, pose for pictures in their colourful race jackets and enjoy a drink with supporters in the riders' clubroom.

For spectators, the thrill was magnified at many of the tracks by the chance to watch the action close up behind barriers which mostly would never pass Health and Safety regulations today. At Rye House, spectators could stand just yards away from the black cinder track and watch four riders competing over four anti-clockwise laps of an oval circuit while leaning on a 'safety barrier' comprising little more than a corrugated iron fence. In time, Peter and his cousin Terry took on the job of painting the safety fence with whitewash.

'You are present at this meeting entirely at your own risk,' was the warning for spectators regularly printed in the Rye House programme notes at each meeting – and with good reason. If fans leaned far enough forward at the Rye House track, they could even touch the riders as they sped by at 70 miles an hour.

Rye House speedway was built in the late 1920s, first as a running track for athletics, then transformed for speedway racing in 1930 with a deep black cinder surface. The Rye House stadium was easily reached by train from London's Liverpool Street station. Fans could step out on to the platform and exit Rye House station with the track just a few minutes' walk away.

By the early 1950s, just as Peter was entering his teens and taking a keen interest in speedway, the Rye House track was thriving with meetings attracting upwards of 4,000 fans, most of whom were extremely knowledgeable about the sport as they followed the fortunes of their favourite riders.

Situated on a 60-acre estate, the track was owned by a star Australian rider by the name of Dickie Case who had represented his country in many speedway test matches and was a member of the Hackney Wick Wolves team before the war.

Case's enthusiastic commitment to speedway was welcomed by the community, and now he began arranging regular weekly practice sessions with himself in attendance to spot riders who showed potential. In addition, on alternate Wednesdays he invited major stars from the Wembley Lions and the Harringay Racers to the track for team practice sessions. It was a big thrill for Peter and his friends on practice days to watch their heroes go through their paces at such close proximity. As a special treat they were occasionally invited to give these top riders a push start.

The sudden death of Peter's uncle Steve could so easily have made Peter fearful of motorbikes in general and ended his interest in speedway there and then. Instead, it helped forge a dream for young Peter Sampson that one day he might step into his uncle's boots, become a speedway rider himself and go some way towards making up for Steve's life being cut so heartbreakingly short. And so, in time, it proved.

Peter's initial training began at the Rye House stadium, which by now was winning a widely recognised reputation within the sport as a breeding ground for up-and-coming riders. Fans who bought programmes at Rye House meetings would find the stadium proudly proclaiming itself as 'The Acknowledged Training Track'.

Consequently, there was no better place than Rye House for Peter to try out his newly acquired speedway bike for the first time – provided he could find a way of getting the bike from his home to the track. 'I had no transport at that time,' he says. 'I had to push the bike and an old army kit bag of equipment a mile and a half to Cheshunt railway station, remain with the bike in the guards van for two stops, then push it along the platform at Rye House, then out of the station and over the bridge into the stadium.'

Peter's first ride was less than memorable. He joined several other riders who were using the track for practice and was given a push-off with just basic instructions that if he wanted to go faster, he should open the throttle, and if he wanted to slow down, he should close the throttle.

Peter set off and was pleased to think he was going quite fast until another rider came past him at high speed while nonchalantly smoking a cigarette. 'I couldn't believe it.' He laughs. 'How could anyone overtake me like that, puffing on a ciggie? I fell off a few times that day and spent as much time sprawled on the track as I did on the bike. Battered and bruised, I then had to make the return train journey pushing my bike back to and from the two railway stations once more to get home.'

Undeterred by his painful introduction to speedway, Peter soon discovered he was hooked on the sport. For any aspiring rider, the path to speedway glory was, and remains, a long, difficult and dangerous one. In Peter's day, new young riders were given a chance to show their potential when they were accorded rides for juniors in the second half of a race meeting. If they managed to score points, they could graduate to the team.

Peter was keen enough to put in the hours of practice required and from a seventeen-year-old rookie he progressed steadily to become good enough to claim the right to ride for the Rye House team.

In his early apprenticeship days Peter made good friends with several other riders, including Colin Pratt, Bill Wainwright, Clive Hitch, Dingle Brown and the Jackson brothers, Peter and Alan, and from the start Peter's great friend Johnny Arthur in particular recognised that Peter not only had the budding talent to become a decent rider but that he also possessed the courage and nerve required to succeed in the sport.

Unselfishly, Johnny was loyally determined to ensure that Peter gave himself every chance of success, even to the extent of warning him repeatedly that girls would be a serious distraction. He continually stressed to Peter that speedway required dedication and focus if he was to achieve anything as a rider.

Johnny Arthur's wife Gladys confirms how protective her husband became of Peter whenever a young girl showed an interest in his speedway protégé: 'You don't need girlfriends. There'll be plenty of time for girls. Just keep to speedway' was his strict advice, she remembers.

Johnny had to accept the inevitable, however. 'Peter was a very good-looking lad,' says Terry Keates. 'In addition to his slim, boyish looks and easy smile, Peter's cheerful, friendly demeanour was an added attraction for the opposite sex.' As Peter himself had begun to find out.

Johnny's guidance about girls was something young Peter didn't altogether care to heed too often; his pals seem to recall. 'All speedway riders were heart-throbs dicing with danger in their leathers,' says close pal John Medcalf, known as 'John the Milk' for his job as a milkman. 'The girls would come flocking. Peter was a good-looking guy and the girls loved him.'

Terry, whose friendship with Peter had broadened after they left school while playing in the same football team together at Rye Park – Peter as a forward with Terry in defence and his cousin Barry in goal – endorses that view: 'We both used to go for the girls whenever we played away.' And Mo Richardson recalls: 'Once he got into speedway, Peter always had girls hanging around him in the pits.'

Despite Johnny Arthur's insistence on total girl-free dedication to speedway, Peter began dating a pretty local teenager by the name of Grace Puddephatt. Grace worked in the rag trade in the city of London but lived not far from Peter at Dobbs Weir, a spot on the River Lea well known for its angling, for its outdoor beauty and for water sports.

The Tudor Dance Hall in Hoddesdon was an early date for the couple but not the first occasion on which Peter had met Grace. Their paths had crossed fleetingly at the wedding party of the sister of mutual friend John the Milk. Clearly, he had made an impression upon her. 'He was lovely looking,' Grace says, 'a pretty good dancer, and a good jiver too.' The dancing lessons had obviously paid off.

Peter's friendship with Grace even won the approval of Johnny Arthur when he started going out with her, and Grace soon realised Peter was becoming very fond of her when he invited her to accompany him to the christening of David King, the baby son of fellow speedway rider Gerry King. It was a statement that they were very much a couple.

Peter and Grace tied the knot on 1 April 1962, and there was much amusement among relatives on both sides that the couple had chosen to get married on April Fool's Day. They both had to put up with plenty of friendly banter and gentle ribbing from their pals about their choice of wedding date, particularly as they had chosen to become man and wife on a Sunday rather than on a Saturday, normally the traditional day for weddings.

There was, however, good reason. Peter was riding speedway on weekdays and Saturdays, and a Sunday suited Grace's side of the family too. Her mother had a family business going back several generations running second-hand book stalls on Farringdon Road in London. 'My mum was very dedicated to her work and wouldn't have been able to attend if we had married on a Saturday,' Grace explains.

Peter had just begun riding for Rye House when his ambitions suffered a serious setback due to an accident at work. By now he had his job driving trucks, wagons and vans for Symonds Engineering and the accident happened while he was helping to unload a lorry stacked with large, heavy eight-inch-thick circular rods of solid steel.

Two colleagues were placing crowbars under the rods to enable Peter to secure a chain underneath in preparation for them to be lifted off the lorry by crane. One of the crowbars suddenly slipped and the rods rolled off, crushing Peter's hand and squashing his fingers in the process. He spent two days being treated in hospital, but the middle finger of his left hand was so badly crushed it required the top of the finger to be amputated.

'I was devastated,' Peter says. 'The biggest upset for me was that I'd just begun speedway riding, and losing the top of that finger was a real blow to my prospects. One of the most important moments in a speedway race is how you first get out of the starting gate. If you can find a fast start and get out in front, you have a big advantage. You have clear vision and you're in with a chance of staying there. If not, after one lap your goggles might be covered in shale and if you took them off so you could see ahead, your eyes and face could be covered too, with loss of vision.

'To achieve a fast start, you needed your left hand to operate the clutch lever with the middle finger the most important of all. Now, all of a sudden, I found that my middle finger couldn't engage properly with the clutch.'

Inevitably the injury temporarily called for a break from speedway to allow Peter's hand to heal. It never entered Peter's head to make an injury claim from his employers. Cheerfully he refused to make a fuss about it and accepted it as just an unfortunate accident. As such, he never considered asking Symonds for compensation. Nevertheless, he was surprised and grateful when he subsequently received a cheque for £30 from the company's insurers.

Peter has always made light of the injury. 'Having worked with animals for forty years, there are some people who would be far happier if I could say that the top of my finger was bitten off by a tiger!' he says cheerfully. 'But the truth is that it was simply down to an unlucky accident.'

Sharing Peter's passion for the sport of speedway was John the Milk, who helped him out as a pit crew mechanic. John spent his mornings on his milk rounds for his father's dairy and by lunchtime he had finished his delivery duties and his day's work was done. That left him free to pick up Peter in his van and set off for speedway meetings together.

'They were fantastic times,' John enthuses. 'We'd go off to a track, race, stop somewhere on the way back for a big fry-up breakfast at two in the morning and get home just in time for me to start on my milk round. Nowhere was too far for us to go. Often we'd get little more than two hours sleep, but we were young and we could take it.'

Peter's former speedway pals are full of happy reminiscences of their adventures – and several misadventures – while accompanying him on the road to and from stadiums all over the country. Terry Keates recalls a day when they were both booked to ride at Middlesbrough speedway and they stacked their two speedway bikes in the back of Terry's small van, which he jointly owned with his father, and headed north. Just outside Middlesbrough the engine started to make a horrendous noise. They managed to nurse the van slowly into the stadium, but an inspection under the bonnet told them it would never make the journey home.

Peter and Terry both rode well on that occasion, but one of the other London riders was involved in a serious crash and was badly concussed. Peter helpfully volunteered to drive him home in the injured rider's brand-new car, a large Ford Zephyr, which allowed the stricken rider to rest up on the back seat. They loaded up his bike on the Zephyr's rear rack, borrowed a heavy-duty tow rope which they attached to Terry's van and, with Terry at the wheel of the van, they set off at 11 p.m. to drive the 235 miles home in the dark.

All was progressing smoothly when the nearside rear wheel suddenly flew off the van and rolled away at speed into the distance, causing everything to come to a screeching halt. Peter and Terry searched everywhere, hampered by the darkness of the night, but were unable to find the missing wheel. They even had the police joining in the search after they arrived on the scene. It took almost an hour before they finally located it in a muddy field and managed to put it back on and secured it by taking nuts off the other wheels.

'We started off again and began to eat up the miles,' says Peter. 'It was a very powerful car. But there came a moment when I was starting to overtake a slow-moving lorry and faced another lorry suddenly coming over the hill straight towards me. I was forced to brake hard, whereupon Terry and the van crunched into the back of the Zephyr. Although the speedway bike on the rack took the bulk of the impact, the front of the van was hanging off.

'Undeterred we carried on, and after another hour or so we finally arrived at the workshop of my house in Cheshunt. It was now daylight, and the damage was finally all too clear to see. The van was effectively a write-off, Terry's father was not a happy man, and the bike on the back of the Zephyr was badly mangled up.

'By now our concussed speedway friend had started to come round. On inspecting his speedbike on the back of his Zephyr he said: "Looking at all that damage to my bike, I don't know how I survived the crash at Middlesbrough." Before we could offer a word of explanation, he jumped in his car and drove back into London!'

Once he became a team rider, Peter quickly learned that speedway could be a time-consuming sport. It required infinite patience to spend hours on the road travelling to various tracks around the country with his bike stashed in his van. This was at a time long before the UK had a network of motorways linking the big cities, and journeys could take more than twice the time they do today.

The hours behind the wheel were tiring, and often challenging too. Peter once drove 330 miles through pouring rain and thick fog to race in Edinburgh only to learn on arrival that the meeting was cancelled because of a waterlogged track. He was obliged to turn around and drive straight back home again, a fruitless round trip of 660 miles.

Another exhausting drive to Cornwall to race at St Austell speedway also ended in frustration. Peter arrived in pouring rain only to see bedraggled supporters streaming away from the stadium, one of whom informed him the meeting had just been cancelled because of the downpour. Without stopping, he swung his van around and drove through the night back to his home in Cheshunt. No sooner had he walked through the door than Grace handed him a recently arrived telegram asking him to come straight back down to St Austell as the meeting had been rearranged for that evening. Peter duly set off back to Cornwall to compete.

As he became a more accomplished speedway rider, Peter moved on from Rye House to Rayleigh, which had the advantage of being just 45 miles away from home. But after a run of exceptionally good performances he was offered the chance to ride either for Newcastle or for the Exeter Falcons the following season. Although both teams were in the top speedway division, he felt Newcastle Diamonds could be a better choice, but it was a decision he soon came to regret. It meant a round trip to meetings of 265 miles each way which took all of ten hours.

The parties which followed every speedway meeting were never less than lively and occasionally legendary. They were wild affairs with music, dancing and liberal quantities of alcohol available. Every stadium had a clubroom where riders and fans alike congregated to dance to the latest hit records and let their hair down.

With no drink-driving laws in place at the time, Peter would often enjoy a few drinks to be sociable after a Rye House meeting on a Sunday night, then drive the vast distance up to Newcastle where he would occasionally stay in digs. After riding for Newcastle, it was customary for him to join fellow riders and supporters for a few drinks in the Newcastle clubroom before leaving at midnight for the long van drive home through the night, arriving in time to have a cup of tea and a chance to snatch a quick breakfast before going straight off to work.

The journeys could be painful, as well as tedious. 'There were times when I'd be hurting after a race. Not badly, but I might have been a bit battered and bruised and hobbling after bashing my leg against a fence, for example. It certainly didn't help me on my drive home.'

One night Peter headed for home accompanied by three other riders, Gil Goldfinch, Bill Andrew and Brian Loach, with Peter driving Gil's van with their four bikes mounted on a trailer behind. By his own admission, Peter was not in the best shape after a very convivial evening drinking in the Newcastle Diamonds clubroom. 'I decided to drive because I was the most sober of us all,' he relates. 'Seat belts weren't compulsory in those days and I wasn't wearing one and as we were approaching Doncaster on a dual carriageway I was starting to feel tired and I leaned against the driver's door. To my horror, the door flew open, and I fell out. I was saved from falling out completely by my feet caught underneath the brake and clutch pedals.

'I was still just about in the van when it careered across the road on to the other side of the dual carriageway. Fortunately, the open door stopped the van from rolling over but our trailer carrying the bikes wasn't so lucky. It flipped over and everything came to a shattering stop just as a lorry was heading right for us. Fortunately, its lights picked out the wreckage and it managed to stop in time. Slowly we managed to right the trailer, get everything back together and set off again. Believe me, it's the quickest I've ever seen three grown men sober up.'

Brian Loach reckons it was a miracle that the four of them didn't all lose their lives. 'I can still remember the moment clearly,' he says. 'There was a series of crash bangs, and I looked up and to my horror I couldn't see anybody behind the steering wheel of the van. Peter had slipped right down in the driver's seat and was hanging out of the door. Then I saw a hand come up and grasp the wheel, followed by Peter dragging himself upright into the driver's seat again.' Brian counts himself extra lucky – three of the speedway bikes were damaged but his was the only one that survived intact.

The gruelling round trips to Newcastle came to an end only when Newcastle's speedway promoter reopened a rebuilt Hackney Wick stadium in 1963 and asked Peter to transfer to the Hackney Hawks. He needed little persuading as Hackney was a mere 35 miles away. But halfway through the season Peter sustained serious injuries in a terrifying crash at Hackney and was unable to take any further part that year.

The crash happened when the footrest of Peter's bike became caught in the chain-fence barrier. The impact spun him around and sent him hurtling into a concrete post, injuring his head, chest and legs. He crashed at such high speed and with such force that incredibly the four-inch concrete post snapped off on impact. Spectators feared the worst for Peter – if a rider comes off his bike in the straight it can be fatal if another rider is following up behind at 70 mph.

Peter was taken to Hackney Hospital but for some reason the hospital didn't pick up on the fact that he had broken his leg, ribs and arm and so they sent him home. Peter was in absolute agony when he came limping up the garden path and he was still in such pain the next morning but still got up and drove to work at Victor Martin in Tottenham. The manager there could see he was in agony and drove him back to Hackney Hospital where, after several X-rays, it was decided that legs, rib and arms were indeed broken.

Typically, much against Grace's better judgement, Peter refused to accept that a broken leg would prevent him from going about his daily life. She says: 'When he came back with his leg in plaster, he altered the pedals on his car so that he could still drive to work. That frightened the life out of me, but he was determined a broken leg in plaster wouldn't stop him working.'

The following year, 1964, Peter might have been back in the speedway saddle more quickly than he eventually was but for his competitive approach on the football field. In an endeavour to get fit, he accepted invitations to play football for a speedway riders team. While in the final stages of recuperation, he turned out for a riders XI in a match against a celebrity XI, which included the singer, stage and film star Tommy Steele at the very height of his fame.

'We played on a very wet, muddy pitch,' Peter recalls, 'and when I tackled Tommy Steele hard in the mud, I twisted both my legs and damaged a cartilage in each knee. One knee required just strapping, but the other was torn. Now I had my other leg in a full-length plaster cast for eight weeks. It was back to the car conversion so I could still drive to work in Tottenham and also work in my workshop at the bottom of the garden each evening.'

Peter was sufficiently recovered to return to speedway for part of the 1964 season. The following year, after a successful trial, he began riding for

Swindon. There he was thrilled to ride as a teammate alongside a legend of the sport, Barry Briggs. Affectionately known as Briggo, the Kiwi rider won the World Individual Championship title four times and appeared in a record seventeen consecutive World Individual finals (1954–1970) and a record eighteen in all. He was a giant of the sport.

Swindon was a different challenge for Peter. He regarded it as a privilege on the occasions he rode as Briggo's team partner. But in a four-rider race, it meant he was not only racing against his partner, the very best rider in the world, the current world champion, but against the opposing team's top two riders as well.

Riding for Swindon had one unexpected benefit for Peter – a kiss from Miss World. At a meeting at Neath speedway in Wales, his win in his first race in the second half took him into the final for the Miss World Trophy. Peter triumphed and received a congratulatory kiss from Ann Sidney, a beauty queen from Poole, Dorset, who was the current Miss World.

While riding alongside Briggo, Peter gained firsthand insight into what went into the making of a world champion. 'Briggo was tall and well built, looked after himself, trained and exercised hard, kept himself fit, ate sensibly, didn't drink alcohol and had a disciplined lifestyle,' he explains. 'His dedication and preparation meant he went out on to the track in the best physical condition possible to give himself the best possible chance of winning his races.

'In contrast, I was probably drinking more than I should and eating the wrong things,' Peter concedes. 'My diet wasn't good, I wasn't going to the gym, and I wasn't as fit as I should have been. Working all day and most evenings didn't help either.

'The top riders trained like footballers. I didn't. There were times when, if it was a bumpy track, I'd be halfway round a third lap, and I was only just about hanging on. I didn't realise how much it took it out of me.'

Peter lacked the complete dedication required to reach the very top. In speedway, first out of the starting gate invariably had the best chance of winning a race and Peter's handling of the throttle at the start was, he admits, a weakness. 'The throttle at the start of a race was a big skillset. But I didn't have the dedication to master getting out of the starting gate like, for example, fellow rider and dear friend Colin Pratt. He practised and practised it and mixed with others who were good at it and learned from them so that he generally won nine out ten of his races.'

All through Peter's speedway years he always had a daytime job as well. But with speedway becoming such an important part of his life, he began to take more and more time off from his job as a driver for Symonds Engineering. To accommodate him, the transport manager offered him the chance to switch roles within the company, to give up driving for Symonds and instead take on a new job working in the factory, where they would allow him to take considerably more time off for speedway.

'I talked it through with John the Welder, and he suggested I give it a go,' Peter says. 'I was given the job of working the fly-press in a line of a dozen men and women all operating the same kind of machines. It was simple work. Basically, we had a dustbin full of widgets on one side, which we had to put under the press and then drop into another dustbin on the other side. After four days I had filled my dustbin with widgets to the brim only for other workers to come up to me and scold me for working too fast! They had filled their bins only half full and told me I'd better go for a walk around the factory. It was the most boring job I ever had and I managed to last only two weeks.'

Relief arrived with the offer of a job working in Tottenham for Victor Martin, a speedway manufacturer and one of the leading companies specialising in supplying engines for speedway bikes, spares and a tuning service. Peter was thus in his element.

Victor Martin himself had died a year or two earlier and his son-in-law Nobby Attwell was now in charge. He employed Peter as a welder, using all the skills Peter had learned from Johnny Arthur in making speedway frames and forks, steel shoes and fuel tanks.

A kind and generous man, Nobby became a significant figure in Peter's life. He was a friend as well as his boss. As they lived not far from each other in Cheshunt, Peter would frequently pick up Nobby in the company's old Ford van and drive him to work. Nobby had nine children of various ages and Peter often found himself arriving at Nobby's house at 7.30 a.m. and having to throw stones at Nobby's bedroom window to wake him up. Once up, Nobby would shout down to Peter that the front door was open and would he kindly give his kids their breakfast while he got ready to leave. 'I'd find myself having to fill nine bowls with cornflakes and milk and we'd be lucky to be back on the road for 9 a.m.,' says Peter. 'It was a great lesson to me to have only two children! Driving up towards north London we occasionally stopped off to have a cup with Nobby's aunty at Edmonton, so we didn't get to work until 10.30, but Nobby never seemed to mind.'

Victor Martin operated from an old Victorian building and Peter was given an upstairs room as his workshop, next to smaller workshops rented out to speedway riders Jack Briggs, Ray Cresp and others. Peter was in a team of just eight working for Nobby and on the floor above was a man called Harry Aldridge who ran a massage and physio business. Several of Harry's clients were celebrities or sports stars, including ice skaters and showjumpers, and on the occasions when they cancelled appointments or failed to turn up, Harry would generously allow Peter to come up for a hot bath and a massage in their place. To return the favour, Peter gave Harry some tomatoes and cucumbers grown by his father-in-law, Frank.

Being such an old building, there was no heating system, which meant Peter working in bitterly cold conditions in the winter. He was amused that Nobby tried to convince the workforce that there was no need to complain about the cold by wearing a short-sleeved shirt and shorts in his office whatever the weather. But a peep through the office keyhole regularly revealed Nobby crouched over an electric fire rubbing his hands together for warmth. Neither Peter nor the other workers were brave enough to challenge Nobby about this.

Nobby liked to close his work premises for lunch between 1 p.m. and 2 p.m., but Peter persuaded him to keep the shop open and let him serve in the shop during lunch hour so as not to keep customers waiting. It was an opportunity for Peter to meet many of the speedway riders of the day.

Not far away from Victor Martin was J.A. Prestwick's, a renowned company specialising in motorcycle engines, and Peter was frequently sent round to pick up various mechanical bits and pieces. It was a sad day for everyone connected with speedway and for Peter himself when Prestwick's closed down. 'On their last day I was sent round in the van on several journeys to collect various engine parts. I can remember the loading bay there and they were so pleased when I helped them load up the van that they gave me four stud crankcases for my efforts.'

Nobby was naturally interested in speedway at New Cross Stadium, and at the conclusion of one speedway meeting he enlisted Peter's help in setting up a firework display. But it almost ended in disaster, Peter remembers. 'We were out in the centre of the green, surrounded by bales of straw, when one of the rockets came down in the middle of the bales and the other fireworks. It could have been carnage, but Nobby and I managed to escape from the burning bales with just blackened clothes and singed hair.'

Along with his job at Victor Martin, Peter continued with his own small welding business at his own home workshop with his pal Johnny Arthur. Inevitably the venture dovetailed neatly with speedway and the sport brought plenty of business Peter's way. But it meant he often spent his evenings welding after he had finished his day job. 'Perhaps what I should have done is told myself firmly: "I'm not going to work, I'm going to be a speedway rider full-time and I'll go and live in a caravan near the track, get to know the promoter and I'll train and practise hard and not stay up welding till midnight every night with Johnny in the large workshop I built at the bottom of the garden."'

The pleasure Peter gained from being a speedway rider was obvious to all. Everyone could see that he adored the sport. He took his riding seriously enough but always with a foremost sense of enjoyment. He was rarely tense before a race and usually full of such nerveless good humour in the build-up that one or two of the most dedicated riders resented his happy-go-lucky demeanour as race time approached. 'Many a time I was in changing rooms with experienced riders, and they would be a bundle of nerves before a race,' he says. 'But I'd be laughing and joking, and even Briggo would have to tell me to stop larking about.

'One young rider who regularly travelled to meetings with me would become so gripped by nerves that he needed us to stop a couple of times on the way so he could be sick by the side of the road. Yes, you need guts for speedway, but nerves didn't seem to affect me much for some reason. I do wonder, however, if I'd been a little more nervous whether I might have gone quicker on the track.'

It was inevitable that Peter would suffer his fair share of bumps and bruises in a high-risk sport which essentially saw big heavy bikes fighting flat out for the same space. Once a rider took a certain line on the track, it took courage to hold that line. Peter had many a spill and knew his limitations. 'I wasn't very good at getting away from the starting gate,' he admits. 'Too often I tried to blast my way around the outside.'

At Rye House Peter once came off the track and crashed head first into the solid safety fence, breaking his nose. In those days the old helmets had webbing on the inside and his helmet slipped down and scraped all the skin off his nose. More seriously, the crash gave him severe concussion.

These days a head injury and concussion in all contact sports is treated with extreme caution and care with an enforced ban on further participation until full assessment and time to recover. But sixty years ago, it was very different. Head injuries were regarded as an occupational hazard at speedway, and riders who suffered concussion were often expected back on the track within days. Peter was no exception. 'Accidents weren't too bad if you fell off and just bounced along the track,' he says. 'But in my day, after a head injury, I could be riding again soon afterwards when I wasn't fully compos mentis.'

Peter's courage was never in doubt, exemplified not least when he accepted an invitation to take part in a stock-car race at New Cross Stadium organised by Nobby Attwell. The requirement for the race was a 10-horsepower car, and Peter found himself an old Ford puddle-jumper which he took into Victor Martin's, stripped down, removed many parts from and painted bright red, then borrowed a tipper lorry to take it to the stadium.

On the day, Peter was all set, when race officials inspected his car and ruled he was unfit to take part as his vehicle had no fitted seat belts. Peter got around the problem by going into the race wearing overalls with the shoulder belts positioned to look as though they were seat belts – one cloth belt stretched around the back of his seat and the other over his shoulder. Very surprisingly it seemed to muster enough approval for him to be allowed to race.

A dozen cars started the race and Peter drove with such skill in avoiding the pile-ups in front of him that going into the latter stages of the race he looked around to find his car was just one of four remaining actively mobile. But then the engine of his car blew up, bringing his race to a halt and with no choice other than to abandon the vehicle. He returned home in the tipper lorry. Peter saw the funny side of that particular outing and decided he was better off racing on two wheels.

Both Steve, in 1962, and Lynn, in 1964, were born at the home of Grace's parents in Andrews Lane, Cheshunt, and Peter was thrilled to be present at the birth of each. 'He wanted to be there,' says Grace. 'He was so proud to become a dad, and he and I both felt it was important for him to be at their births.'

With his children's arrival, the responsibility for the welfare of his family now brought about a different mindset for Peter every time he sat astride a speedway bike at the starting gate waiting for the race to begin. 'My son Steve was born in the year I broke my leg while riding at Hackney,' he points out. 'So now, all of a sudden, there were different things going through my head at the track.'

After lengthy consideration, Peter decided he was ready to call time on the sport he loved. He was at an age at which many speedway riders were just starting out, but his cousin Terry Keates had also called it a day The demands of his daytime job working for Victor Martin's coupled with the gruelling travel schedule for speedway had become impractical. He was spending too long behind the wheel and not enough time with his young family, and his fatherly instincts told him it was time to stop risking life and limb on the track and spend more time with his wife and kids. He says: 'By the end of the 1965 speedway season, I was twenty-five years old and I felt I was not progressing in the way I would have liked. Also, the number of trips to hospitals I had been making from various speedway crashes was beginning to register with me and I felt the family must come first.'

Two instances hastened his retirement. The first occurred when he was on the last lap of a race and was trailing last of the four riders. A glimmer of an opportunity opened up to speed through a gap between the rider lying third and a safety fence. 'It would be a bit of prestige to come third rather than last and it would mean more money,' Peter says. 'So, I went for it, my foot caught in the safety fence, which was like chicken wire, and I ripped down 100 yards of fencing and tore my leathers. It was then I wondered if it had all been worth it just to try and come third rather than last.'

The second instance which beckoned Peter towards retirement was the day he was walking down his garden path to place his bike in his van ready to drive down to Swindon to race. 'As I was coming down the path, my next-door neighbour, Reg Clayton, was in his garden bedding in a few new plants and dead-heading his roses. He was happy as Larry, and I was facing a long drive to Swindon. I looked at Reg and wished for a moment that I was living like that.'

Peter went out of the sport with his head held high, and with the respect of his peers as a rider. He also left with the gratitude of many for the time and effort he unselfishly and generously put in all week preparing the bikes of other riders for their races. It was commonly felt that Peter would have achieved a lot more success if he had devoted more time to working on his own bike.

The sport of speedway is renowned for its camaraderie and Peter retains many warm friendships in the speedway fraternity that have lasted for more than sixty years. He has so many fond and lasting memories of his speedway years, not least his first experience of flying. He boarded a plane at Southend airport to fly to Amsterdam with Bill Wainwright and other speedway riders along with their bikes and equipment for a speedway meeting in Nijmegen in the Netherlands close to the border with Germany.

Inevitably, due to his involvement in a sport fraught with danger, Peter has some sad memories as well as good, of fellow riders who suffered life-changing injuries or lost their lives on the track. Every fatality was tragic for the sport but one particularly sad loss was an Australian by the name of Dave Wills. The young rider from 'down under' had saved up every penny from his job as a truck driver to leave his home in Adelaide to travel 12,000 miles to pursue his dream of riding in the UK.

Peter befriended Dave when the young Aussie lodged at the Globe Hotel, Wormley, not far from Peter's home. He came and helped out most evenings at the workshop at the bottom of Peter's garden. Dave soon rode his way into the West Ham team but tragically lost his life at the Custom House Stadium while racing for the Hammers against their greatest rivals, Hackney.

The following week the West Ham programme of 29 June 1965 carried a tribute to Dave Wills, and all speedway riders who had died in the sport, with the citation: 'Speedway can be wicked and cruel, it's a man's game, and they know that, they accepted that, how were they to know the dice was loaded against them.'

Dave's death was especially sad for Peter and had a profound effect. 'It certainly focused the mind the next time I raced after a death on the track when the stadium would be hushed for a minute's silence.

'Apart from the speedway friends I lost, I have several others who today are in wheelchairs. Some of them were badly injured when they were young and they have now spent three times as many years of their lives in a wheelchair as they did without one. So I do know I was lucky.

'All through my time as a rider I was Joe Average,' is Peter's assessment of his speedway career, although rivals and team mates would rate him much more highly. 'I wanted to be a speedway rider, I consider myself fortunate to become one, and I was fortunate enough to be in good teams,' he says. 'I rode with and against some of the very best riders of the day, and I'm very proud that I was in the same team as legends like Mike Broadbank and Barry Briggs when he was world champion. They were both heroes of mine. And I can say truthfully that I once beat Briggo in a race. It was, however, just the once – but only, he says, because his bike had clutch trouble!'

Briggo is in no doubt about Peter's ability. Now a lifelong friend, he says, 'Peter was a good rider, no question, and he was brave and enjoyed it. Some people become riders for fun, others for the glory, and others to make it their life. But I think Peter was probably too nice a man to make it to the very top. I was surprised when he first took on a zoo. Caring for animals is a bit different from pistons and crankshafts. But I'm not surprised he's made an incredible success of it. You can see his heart is totally in it.'

If there's one regret for Peter about his speedway years, it's that he never became a champion. 'If I'd had what I've got about me now, I think I could have been,' he states.

Peter and Rocky

Peter with his mother Gladys Sampson, 1939

Peter's father Sidney Sampson
in the army during WWII

Peter in the garden
at Walton Road,
Hoddesdon –
approx. 3 years old

Peter's grandad Charles Ison's cycle shop in Rye Road, Hoddesdon

Hoddesdon Rye Park Football Club – Peter with his cousins Terry Keates and Barry Oakman (goalie)

Steve Ison, when he rode for Haringey Speedway

Peter and his Morris 1000 van for travelling to and from speedway meetings

Peter riding for Rye House at Eastbourne

Peter and his best mate,
the mechanic John the Welder
(John Arthur)

Swindon Robins 1965

Peter with his friend John the Milk (John Medcalf) in the Speedway Museum

Peter's daughter Lynn and son Steve with their squirrel monkey friends

Sampson Coaches and Travel Agency, Turners Hill, Cheshunt

The great team at Sampson Coaches and Travel

Sampson depot at Dobbs Weir, Hoddesdon

Sampson subsidiary companies Alexandra and Enfieldian

Grace, Lynn and Steve at the opening of the Brimsdown (North London) depot

Fleetville Garage and MOT testing station, Hoddesdon

The old Broxbourne Zoo

Yvonne with Bobby

Bobby the lion prior to moving to new green enclosure, 1986

Steve, Sally the dog and Charlie the monkey all lived in the caravan

The first toilet block on car park 1, built by Ray Chapman and Peter, became meerkat toilets!

Peter and his first grandson, Aaron

Rachael with two of the many hand-reared cubs

Peter with Aaron, Tyler, Cameron and Scott, feeding Rocky

The film studio arrived and sponsored the new lion habitat – Lion King!

Peter and his beloved Rocky

Peter and Malcolm Dudding (WHF–BCS), Marley Farm

Allen and Pauline Richardson, lifelong friends who now live in Australia, at WHF with Peter

Peter, Lynn and Brian Kane, trustee of WHF, (now The Big Cat Sanctuary) with two very rare Amur leopard cubs born at the sanctuary

Lynn and Peter tickling their first tapir calf born at PWP

Peter and good friend Pete James in Singapore on a zoo tour

Peter, Colin and Rocky

Peter's love of motorbikes, and speedway in particular, has never waned. After he finished riding, he helped run the speedway training school at Rye House with his cousin Terry for several years and then helped to create the National Speedway Museum, which has its own special pride of place at Paradise Wildlife Park (PWP), now renamed Hertfordshire Zoo (HZ), with a memorial garden to those who lit up the sport in years gone by.

By a strange anomaly, despite having ridden like the wind around all the major speedway tracks in the country, Peter did not pass his motorcycle road test until he was nearly seventy years old. He possessed a licence to drive cars and vans, buses and coaches, and even HGV lorries – but never a motorbike licence.

His lack of a motorcycle licence had never seriously troubled Peter until a friend, Mick Lewis, offered him a ride on his brand-new, powerful 850cc Triumph Bonneville bike. Without a licence, Peter had to decline but jokingly asked, 'Can you get me one, too?' When he did just that, Peter knew it was time to get himself a licence so he could legitimately ride it.

Together with zoo colleague Steve Saunders he enrolled at a motorbike training school in St Albans, where, for a couple of hours on three separate days, they went through training and practice procedures to prepare for their tests in gale-force winds and rain.

Peter had to travel to Harlow to take the theory part of the test and he stayed up very late on the night before in order to swot up on the Highway Code. 'I arrived at the test centre to find around twenty young people all waiting to take the same test as me. The examiner announced to us all that we had one hour in which to complete the test, and I figured I might struggle in comparison with the others because the test was set on a computer and they were likely to be far more comfortable with a keyboard and screen than me. But I completed the test in just twenty minutes while all the others were the ones who appeared to be struggling.'

Peter passed with 99 marks out of 100 and, on speaking to the examiner afterwards, he was informed that in reality he could just as easily have given him a 100 per cent pass mark.

If the theory exam was easy for Peter, the practical test astride a motorcycle on the roads around St Albans proved to be tricky. The examiner issued

Peter with an earpiece and explained he would ride behind him on another motorbike and give him instructions through his microphone.

'So off we went,' says Peter. 'I felt it was all going extremely well until I was instructed to take the next left turning. Sadly I didn't take the turning he wanted and so now I was lost. Over my earpiece I heard him tell me to stay where I was and that he would come and find me – which he did. There followed a debate between us over which turn I should have taken and while we were arguing the point he then informed me that time was running out. If I didn't complete the test within the time limit, I would fail.'

Peter turned his motorbike around as quickly as possible, successfully underwent a braking test and then set off to ride down a long dual carriageway with the examiner on his bike behind him. 'Knowing time wasn't on my side I went flat out, but keeping just within the speed limit, only to hear in my earpiece the examiner complaining he was unable to keep up with me. As I was up against the clock I felt that was hardly my problem.'

Safely back at the test centre within the time limit, Peter was unsure if he had done enough to pass. Given the dispute over the left turn and the examiner's grumble about his inability to keep up with Peter, it would have been no surprise if he had failed him. 'In a stern voice, the examiner said he needed to speak to me in his office. I feared the worst, but once in his office he congratulated me on riding the motorbike extremely well and told me I had passed.'

Now a bona fide rider, the gleaming new 850cc Triumph Bonneville awaited, hidden in his daughter Lynn's garage. 'He knew I wouldn't approve,' says his partner Rachael smiling broadly at the mischief. 'I was horrified when I found out. "What are you thinking?" I told him. "If you come off this bike you'll break into a thousand pieces."

'The motorcycle licence was the only one Peter hadn't acquired, so I could understand that he was determined to have it. But I banned him from using the bike. I allowed him to ride around the park but he fell off once and the bike was so heavy he couldn't lift it back upright again. I think he probably went out on the bike on the sly,' Rachael adds with good humour.

The depths of winter were far from ideal for Peter's first few rides on the open road, and ironically his greatest danger astride the bike was the bronchial pneumonia he contracted while riding out in the rain.

'All the training and practising I'd done in the pouring rain left me with bronchitis,' he says ruefully. 'The weather was still wet, windy and cold and I had Rachael's words ringing in my ears, telling me "You'll kill yourself." To be fair, I did have a few narrow misses. But after a while common sense prevailed and I sold the Bonneville to one of our team at Paradise.'

Peter has never lost touch with speedway – and perhaps he is even more prominently linked to the sport now than when he himself was a rider. He remains a figurehead for the sport thanks to his offer to have a national speedway musem built in the grounds of Paradise Wildlife Park.

The idea for a museum was first suggested to him in 2004 by Dingle Brown, a former speedway rider for Rayleigh Rockets in the 1960s who went on to become a speedway manager and promoter. At first Peter was not convinced the grounds of a wildlife park was the right setting for a speedway museum. But at a meeting attended by several speedway stalwarts he changed his mind and agreed not only to have the museum built on the PWP site but offered to contribute financially to the project and help with labour and equipment costs.

Overall, the bill was estimated at £50,000 and Peter generously stated that if others could raise 50 per cent of the costs, he would make up the balance.

Former West Ham rider George Barclay and his partner Linda volunteered to spearhead the fundraising drive and did so with tireless determination and enthusiasm. They travelled to all the speedway tracks in the UK to go around the crowd with buckets asking for donations at each venue. Within a period of six months, they had raised half of the required amount, which was enough for Peter to give the go-ahead for building to commence.

Within a speedway season they were well on their way to reaching their target. Peter's in-house Paradise building team had been hard at work preparing and concreting a large base for the new build. Mick Lewis, a friend at M & M Engineering, then built and erected the very large steel framework and supplied the insulated cladding. Electrical work followed and a gas heating system was fitted.

The museum opened on 23 April 2007, brimming with a vast collection of bikes, helmets, jackets, cups, trophies, programmes and other donated memorabilia from around the world from the golden days of speedway and ice racing. Set up as a charity as the National Speedway Museum, it quickly became a must-visit venue for speedway riders and fans past and present and for everyone connected to the sport.

In collaboration with the association of speedway riders, the museum has evolved into one full charity, the World Speedway Riders' Association. The National Speedway Museum was already a charity, and Peter amalgamated this with the World Speedway Riders' Association to become one charity. It continues to be a hugely popular venue for visitors, and an inaugural Bikers in Paradise day in June 2009 became a two-wheeled extravaganza with more than 700 motorcycles lined up across the car parks. The annual Celebration of Speedway and other events attract huge numbers. Past riders are remembered with a special event in the memorial garden. As the National Speedway Museum expanded, Mac and Elaine MacDougal played an integral part. On the outside of the museum, there is a mural 30 feet (9 metres) long depicting speedway through the ages, designed and undertaken by Mac.

Hosting biker days at the park, Peter can regularly find many hundreds of motorcyclists heading to Paradise. An occasional visitor has been Eddie Kidd, the famous British motorcycle stunt rider whose exploits included jumping over the Great Wall of China on a motorbike. Eddie lived close to PWP and from time to time Peter would carry out some of his bike repairs and welding for him.

Most recently Peter was able to stage a day at the speedway museum devoted to Ove Fundin, the legendary five-times world speedway champion from Sweden, who made the trip over with his wife at the grand age of ninety. On his visit he was thrilled to take the opportunity to hand-feed one of Peter's tigers.

CHAPTER FIVE
Wheels in Motion

'I arrived into the coach and bus business by accident. I knew nothing about it when I started out. But life is a learning curve'

— *Peter Sampson*

All the while he was a speedway rider and working for Victor Martin, Peter Sampson was additionally running a small business of his own from the shed at the bottom of his garden. There he carried out car and motorcycle repairs and, of course, welding, with his great pal Johnny Arthur, whom he rated as 'the greatest welder in the world' – a reputation that was widely acknowledged by all who knew him.

John the Milk remembers: 'Peter's garden workshop was like a little factory. Lots of us would gather down there every single night. Peter and Johnny would be working away welding, making fuel tanks and repairing speedway bike frames, as well as steel shoes, which speedway riders needed on the track for steadying the left foot on their bikes as they broadsided around the bends.'

Even after a day at work at Victor Martin, it was not uncommon for Peter and Johnny to be welding till midnight and beyond, sometimes way into the very small hours, and yet still be ready to go off to work at 7.30 a.m. Grace accepted that their garden shed was not just a workshop but also served as a social gathering for Peter and his friends. 'It meant that ours was a house full of men every night,' she says. 'It wasn't unusual to find a dozen men in the front room waiting for Peter to come home after work. John and Pete were always working away welding till midnight while I got on with some dressmaking.'

At the end of the 1965 speedway season, Peter felt ready to leave Victor Martin to strike out on his own by setting up a repair and welding business, Sampson Engineering Ltd. He was able to transfer the workshop from his garden to a large workshop he rented at a small nursery in Nazeing in Essex, six miles away from his home. This workshop was spacious enough to accommodate four cars at a time for him to work on, enough to create a viable business.

On notifying Victor Martin director Nobby Attwell that he was about to leave his employ and set up on his own, Peter was in for a double surprise. Nobby firstly revealed that he was about to sell up his own business and emigrate to New Zealand, and he then came up with a remarkable offer: if Peter was prepared to emigrate with him to set up a joint business in New Zealand, then he would pay all the costs of moving the Sampson family to the land of the long white cloud.

It was a tempting proposition and a rare, life-changing opportunity, but one which Peter knew in his heart he had to refuse. It would have meant a major upheaval for his family, his children, Steve and Lynn, were both very young; he was largely looking after his mother Gladys; and he had to consider what impact a move to New Zealand would have on Grace and her own mother and father.

Peter was flattered by Nobby's approach but turned it down and says: 'I do wonder what would have happened if I'd accepted his offer.' Nobby duly moved to New Zealand and became a successful strawberry farmer and, sadly for Peter, they lost contact. He learned many years later that Nobby had died after falling into a fire while burning garden waste on his land.

On leaving Nobby's employ, Peter now grabbed the chance to expand his Nazeing operation into a business of his own. As well as preparing vehicles for

MOT testing, he now had the premises in which to carry out body repairs and resprays with the aid of a very large compressor to give him the air for the spray gun. The repair side of his operation began to go so well that he also decided to cease working with John the Welder at the bottom of the garden. The parting was entirely amicable as John himself was in turn able to relocate to larger workshops in Pindar Road, Hoddesdon. In later years Peter also build his own MOT garage and workshops in Pindar Road.

At first Peter was unaware that the owner of the Nazeing workshop he was renting happened to live on the same premises in a bungalow just 200 yards away and that his home was served by the same electricity circuit as the workshop. Whenever Peter started up his compressor, the picture on the owner's television screen had a habit of shrinking to just two inches square, prompting a visit from the owner irately demanding to know what he was up to. Peter soon learned to keep a keen ear out for the first sounds of the owner's footsteps striding angrily down the path from his bungalow to his workshop to confront him. If he was quick, Peter had just about enough time to switch off the compressor and summon up a look of sympathetic bewilderment when the owner arrived to announce he was having trouble with his TV and to ask Peter whether he was the cause of the annoying malfunction.

It was from these small beginnings at Nazeing that Peter entered the coaching business which was to dominate his life for the next three decades – and it all happened quite by chance.

One morning a Mr Warner, who ran a limousine taxi hire business and provided cars for weddings and funerals, brought in one of his cars for repairs to a damaged rear wing. 'He asked me if he could pick up his repaired car in time to do a school round. I asked what that was and he said he took several children in his car from their homes to school every day and then collected them again in the afternoons.

'I said I would get the wing repaired and sprayed with an undercoat of paint so he could pick up the car later that day and return it the following day for the topcoat respray. When Mr Warner duly returned the following day, he told me he intended to give up his driving contract with the school and asked if I would be interested in taking it over. He said the contract paid £20 per week (£4 per day), which seemed exceptional to me at the time, then told me I would need to apply to Hertfordshire County Council (HCC) to take over his contract to take children to and from a special needs school in Broxbournebury.'

Peter figured he would be up for the job because he already owned a completely renovated car at the time, and when HCC sent him through the relevant application form he just filled it in without reading the contract properly and sent it off.

Peter happened to be in hospital recovering from injuries he had received from his speedway days when Grace brought him a letter from HCC informing him his application had been successful. That was the good news, but it was tempered by the bad news that the contract stipulated it was for a 12-seater minibus – with driver and escort. 'That was an important lesson, always read the paperwork,' Peter says ruefully.

'I could have written on the back of a postage stamp what I knew about minibuses, coaches and driving licences and how the system worked. With my utter lack of knowledge, I managed to purchase an old works minibus from Bell & Webster, a firm based in Hoddesdon, and I completely refurbished it. I resprayed it, fixed the brakes, lights and steering and reupholstered the work benches in the back for the workmen, so the vehicle now looked pristine. I then found out I had to apply for a Public Service Vehicle driving licence and I duly applied.

'In those days PSV tests were held at New Scotland Yard in London. So, in my suit and tie, I set off for London with a copy of my car driving licence. I recall going into the building to be told to wait outside for the examiner to come out to conduct my PSV test, and when he emerged I was in for a shock. He looked at my minibus and said, "You won't be able to take your test in that." I initially thought he was having a joke with me so I laughed, perhaps foolishly. He explained my vehicle did not meet the requirements for a public service vehicle: the roof was not high enough for people to stand; it had no emergency exit, no fire extinguisher and no first aid kit. The list went on and on. I can only put it down to another lesson learned in life.

'The following day, I started to look around for a suitable vehicle. In Ware in those days there was a firm of coach builders called Thurgood's and they had what was a Trojan make minibus. Without doubt, it was the ugliest thing I had ever seen, but it could serve my needs as it was a 12-seater. They informed me it needed a new test and some mechanical work which could be carried out at Arlington's garage in Ponders End, north London. The vehicle was delivered there and when I went to visit to speak with the garage manager, I found to my surprise that some apprentices I had worked with many years previously at Haslemere Garage were now working there as skilled fitters. I told them the tale of why I needed the minibus and they said they would make it like new for me, which they did. At the time, it was up for sale for £350. After much trying, even though I had a small deposit, I could not obtain finance or hire purchase so it was back to the drawing board.

'The day for me to start the school contract was looming; I still had no minibus and no PSV driving licence. In checking through the phone book, I found a coach company near Hatfield and on speaking to them, they were prepared to hire me a coach for a few hours in which to take my test. I went over there to find it was not a minibus they were offering to loan me but a full size 45-seater coach. That was far from ideal, but I knew my driving experience with lorries at Symonds Engineering would hold me in good stead, and I managed to have forty minutes of successful practice driving the coach prior to meeting the examiner at the designated location.

'Again, I was in my suit and tie and had studied the Highway Code from front to back. A really smart examiner came on board with his trilby hat, looked at my car licence, went through the various forms and said he would sit in a seat near the rear and shout out instructions – "left here, right there." Then he asked me to reverse, not a simple reverse, but round a sharp corner and up a hill. I thought this could be a disaster but fortunately, it didn't go too badly. We completed the driving test then went through the Highway Code and I ticked all the boxes. He then said to me, "If you don't mind my asking, how long have you been driving large coaches?" I told him approximately two hours. He said he was very pleasantly surprised, told me I had passed my test, and gave me a full PSV driving licence. Finally he asked if I'd mind if he gave me some advice: "When you go around roundabouts, please take it carefully, as you wouldn't want people sliding off their seats." That advice still sticks with me today.'

Relieved at having passed, Peter pulled out a bottle of Scotch whisky to give to the examiner as a gesture of thanks. His exact words, Peter recalls, were: 'I'm pleased to accept, but if you had offered this to me before the test I would have had to have failed you.'

At this point in his life Peter and Terry were still tying up the loose ends of their speedway training school when Bill Matisson, a good friend who had become increasingly involved in speedway, expressed an interest in buying the bikes and equipment. In real terms this was not worth a great deal as most were semi-wrecked, but Bill knew Peter was trying to buy a small mini-coach and offered him £100 to carry on servicing and repairing the bikes for a further twelve months. Peter was more than happy to agree as that gave him a deposit for his minibus.

On scanning several commercial motor magazines Peter located a Bedford minibus in south London suitable for his needs. 'The following day, I made arrangements to visit the garage's car sales, an experience I found to be akin to dealing with Arthur Daley, the Cockney wheeler-dealer from the hit TV series *Minder*. I explained I had a bona fide contract to drive kids to school but at this moment in time I could not get hire purchase. The dealer was more than happy with my story and I paid him £100 deposit and he said he would stand the balance himself and we worked out a monthly payment programme. The total cost of the small bus was £325 and I recall getting a very nice letter from him when I made my final payment saying it was good to do business with me and if need be, he would be very happy to make similar arrangements again.

'The good news was that now I had a licence to drive buses and coaches, I had my own minibus and was ready to start the first day of our school contract picking up children with disabilities. It was a total family concern with my mother as the escort. The schoolchildren were a great bunch of kids, irrespective of their disabilities, and this was the first day of more than thirty years for me in the bus and coach business.'

Many years later Peter purchased the Warners Limousine and Car Hire business and for a few years carried on supplying cars for weddings and funerals.

* * *

Prior to starting the school bus contract in 1966, Peter and Grace planned to take their two children to the West Country for their first family holiday. While almost the entire UK population was watching England playing Germany at Wembley on TV in the final of football's World Cup, Peter was popping in and out of his house in Clarendon Road busily stripping down the engine of the newly acquired minibus parked in the road outside. He was due to drive the family to a farm site near Newquay in Cornwall the following day, and it was 10 p.m., five hours after England had won the Cup, before Peter had finished replacing parts and putting the engine back together again.

The holiday proved to be a welcome seaside break, but Peter's main memory is of the moment he feared his toddler son Steve had gone missing. The family were enjoying time on the beach when Grace suddenly alerted Peter that their boy was nowhere to be seen. He had disappeared. Peter ran frantically up and down the shore in both directions desperately looking for his son. When there was no sign of him, he waded into the sea up and down the coastline fearing the worst until Steve was eventually discovered playing happily with another family at the back of the beach. 'It's embedded in my mind, every parent's nightmare,' he says. 'But what a relief.'

***

Having begun his contract with Broxbournebury Special School, Peter soon expanded into catering for small private coach parties. He also tendered for more school contracts and secured one that this time required a 37-seat coach. Thumbing through trade magazines he spotted an advertisement for a 1953 Thurgood Bedford petrol coach for sale from Bishops Stortford firm Don's Coaches and he travelled to view it with son Steve, who was four at the time. 'I met with the owner, Jim Hale, one of life's nice guys, and he invited me to take it for a test drive, which I undertook. I must admit it wasn't the prettiest or the nicest coach I'd ever seen but at £125 it was perfect for me. In fairness to Mr Hale, he agreed I could pay him £25 a month for the coach and he threw in a surplus office desk and a filing cabinet with the sale and also gave me private hire work with the coach. What was interesting for me was I saw at his depot that he had a fleet of half a dozen coaches which were like new and immaculate. So, even then it set me dreaming that perhaps one day ...'

The first major development of the business came courtesy of Grace. 'We reckoned that if Grace could pass her minibus test, she could take on the school contract while I drove the recently purchased coach on another school contract. The good news was that Grace passed her test, and several years later she took a second test in one of our old double-decker Bristol half-cab buses with a crash gearbox and no power steering. Without doubt, it was one of the most difficult things to drive,' Peter stresses, 'but Grace comfortably passed.

'Locally in Cheshunt I had made friends with a man called Danny Oxley who had built a new workshop in Fieldings Road, Cheshunt. It was large enough to take commercial vehicles and he also had a small yard so he agreed that I could park my coaches there for free if I did his welding for him for free. We shook hands and the deal was done.'

Peter soon realised that coaches with petrol engines were not ideal so he bought a relatively old Bedford 300 diesel engine from a local breaker's yard and set about carrying out the conversion in Danny's workshop. 'As you can imagine, it was a tough job. I had to make all new engine mountings, change the gearbox and alter the prop shaft among many other things. But after a week of constant work I sat in the driving seat, pressed the button, turned the key and it roared into life. It was another great learning curve.

'Business was starting to prosper with more private coach hire with trips here and there far and wide, so I then arranged a meeting with Arlington's Coach Sales at Potters Bar and purchased a 45-seater coach, but again with a petrol engine. I decided I'd also convert it to diesel and this time I bought a Leyland engine, which at the time was more powerful than the Bedford. Once again it was a mammoth task to convert it to diesel but, as before, we turned the key and the engine burst into life.

'As my small fleet was growing, I needed a driver and I approached Grace's father, Frank. He agreed for us to arrange for him to take his coach driving test, and after a few weeks of training, I was pleased when Frank passed. In real terms he was our first employee.

'When I look back with hindsight, the time, energy and expense I put into converting the two coaches from petrol to diesel was not the greatest of ideas. But at that time it was affordable, and it taught me all about diesel engines, which stood me in good stead for the future. I don't think anyone prior or since has carried out these engine conversions in coaches. So it remains a first.'

By 1968 Danny Oxley was approaching retirement age and he asked Peter if he would like to buy his workshop and yard. 'The price was £16,000,' Peter remembers. 'That seems unbelievable now, but my accountant at the time foolishly advised against it. In effect, that was very bad advice – a lesson learned, do it your way! It put me in a difficult position as I then had to find another location for parking my coaches and minibuses.'

As luck would have it Peter found it in the next-door depot and yard in Fieldings Road owned by a man called Gerry Stacey, who had a large fleet of lorries. The two men shared a common love of speedway and over the years they became great friends. Gerry conveniently took his coach driving test in one of Peter's coaches and Peter equally conveniently took his HGV lorry test in one of Gerry's vehicles and passed.

In addition to the use of Gerry's yard, Peter managed to rent a railway arch at Theobalds Grove railway station at Waltham Cross as it proved just big enough to fit a coach inside. But he quickly discovered it was prone to flooding in heavy rain and he needed to look elsewhere. He arranged a 9 a.m. meeting with Cheshunt Urban District Council's financial director Brian Seaton and arrived suited and booted on the dot at his large office. 'As I sat down, Mr Seaton opened two large wooden doors to a massive drinks cabinet,' Peter remembers, 'and he invited me to join him with a large whisky. Even though it was just nine o'clock in the morning, it would have been rude of me to refuse.

'After a while Harry Bishop, the chief executive of the council, came to join us and more whisky was consumed between the three of us. I explained I was local to Cheshunt and ran coaches taking local children to school and they offered me the opportunity to rent a large parcel of land in Waltham Cross, Hertfordshire. It had a yard which sounded ideal, and I left the meeting slightly worse for wear but pleased I had a new location for our coaches and had met two very special men with whom I went on to have long and enjoyable friendships.'

The Waltham Cross yard was more like a cleared building site but large enough for Peter's purposes, and he set about putting up fences, making large gates, and buying two sizeable old walk-in laundry lorries, converting one into an office and the other into a drivers' room. He used old materials, box steel and corrugated steel sheets to make a small workshop and had electricity, water and telephone lines laid on. Peter was joined at the yard by Scottie Weeks, a friend of many years' standing who had been a special friend of his late uncle, speedway rider Steve Ison, and together they worked on stripping down the very large coach engines. 'That was quite a job,' Peter says. 'Some of the pistons were the size of dinner plates.'

By 1969, just four years after starting up, Peter's fleet had grown substantially and he was now trading as Sampson Coaches. Over the next three years as he took on more contracts for schools and works, his fleet increased to ten vehicles, including two minibuses, which required the recruitment of new drivers, including Peter's friend John 'the Milk' Medcalf, who had now passed his coach driving test. John would help out in the afternoons after completing his milk rounds.

Soon Peter began operating coach tours and weekends away, provided they were private bookings. Around the same time, in 1970, Peter purchased a double-fronted shop with two flats above and one at the side. After a great deal of alterations and changes, he opened one side of the shop as Sampson Coaches and Travel Ltd and to help pay the bills he rented the other side of the shop to Dave Hewitt and Pete Sale, who specialised in radios and TVs. In the coming years, Peter's son Steve and daughter Lynn each owned one of the flats above the shop.

Business was thriving, but it wasn't all work and no play. When time allowed, Peter started going to watch Tottenham Hotspur football matches with his cousin Terry at Spurs' old White Hart Lane stadium and, with son Steve beginning to play a good standard of football, Peter set up a team of his own with the help of his neighbours, the Milburn family, and another neighbour, Sean Noonan, whose son Kevin was also in the team. They named the team Clarendon FC after their own road and together they purchased the shirts and kit. 'It was my first stint at being a football manager,' Peter says proudly. 'Steve and all the other boys played exceptionally well and Clarendon FC carried on for several seasons.'

Expanding still further, Peter opened his first coach booking office/shop, with Margaret Boyd becoming the first full-time travel shop employee, with two more staff added as the business started to grow.

'After a while, I could see the opportunity of applying to be full-time travel agents,' Peter says. 'To achieve this, I had to sit several exams on travel, coaches and tours, which I am pleased to say I passed. We were then fully inspected by the Association of British Travel Agents (ABTA) and we were proud to be accepted as full members. Interestingly, it was ten to fifteen years since a new member had joined. We then paid some compensation to Hewitt and Sale to move out. Fortunately, there was an empty shop opposite for them to move in to. For our travel and coach business, we now had both sides of the large shop. To help reduce the operating costs, we let off part of our shop to the local school of motoring and also to the local insurance brokers.

'Gradually we took on full-time travel staff as the travel business was really starting to take off. We appointed John Warren as the manager of the travel side and Margaret Boyd continued as manager of the coach booking side. As we had a main road frontage, we had a great opportunity to place blackboards outside advertising not just coaches but also our holidays.'

The ABTA travel licence meant that Peter could sell not only his own trips but package holidays as well. This quickly led to an important business link with Freddie Laker, the English airline entrepreneur who famously revolutionised transatlantic travel during the 1970s by taking on the major established airlines as the first low cost, no frills carrier. Peter soon became the biggest UK agent for Laker's tours, which offered a week's package holiday to the US for £99.

By its very nature, sending coaches over the Channel to European destinations generally proved a challenge for Sampsons. It was one which Peter accepted with relish, but not always with the smoothest of outcomes when vehicles broke down.

Further expansion of Peter's coach business followed in 1971 when Peter bought his first brand-new, full-size 50-seater coach for £12,500 (£375,000 at today's prices). The Turners Hill premises had the advantage of affording much-needed space for office accommodation. Up until then, the hallway of Peter's home had effectively been his office.

* * *

In 1973, shortly after adding a new 57-seat Leyland coach to his fleet, Peter embarked on a journey he realised from the very start was never going to be easy – to southern Poland, or the Polish People's Republic as it was then known. For the very first time he would be taking the new coach, packed to capacity with fifty-seven speedway fans, behind the Iron Curtain. In it he would take the party over the Channel, first through France, then Belgium and on through East Germany to Poland. It was an international excursion very dear to his heart because the ultimate destination was Poland's Silesian Stadium in Chorzow, near Katowice, and the occasion was the 1973 Individual Speedway World Championship, which would determine who was the best rider in the sport.

The adventure required meticulous pre-planning. Peter had to acquire the necessary visas for all fifty-seven passengers, for himself, his coach crew, Bob and Vic, and John the Welder, who would be travelling with him. Various other certificates and permits were also required, hotels had to be booked, and Peter needed a trip up to London to buy Polish currency, the zloty, on behalf of everyone. There he purchased £1,000's worth of zloty at an exchange rate of ten zloty to the pound to pay for fuel en route and to provide enough spending money for his party of fans to enjoy themselves.

'The journey to Poland was an absolute nightmare,' Peter remembers. 'It was a case of getting past aggressive guards bristling with guns at numerous checkpoints, bribing people with cigarettes, driving down dark, murky and scary streets and being aggressively confronted by KGB officials in belted raincoats and trilbies. We were delayed for hours at every single checkpoint.'

Life for Communist Poland's inhabitants meant being closely watched, censored and deprived of basic necessities, and it all came as a shock to

Peter's party as they peered out of the coach windows – little old ladies dressed in black, pulling carts filled with their meagre possessions along bumpy old roads, and no ambulance coming to the rescue when a crash was witnessed on the road. A motorcyclist who'd been badly injured in an accident was seen to be just carted away in a pick-up truck. It was a shocking sight for the fifty-seven motorcycle-mad passengers.

'Because of all the delays we arrived very late in the evening,' Peter recounts. 'Our hotel was dark, dingy and unwelcoming. Everything was very basic and minimal and there were no lifts to the upper floors. When I walked into my room the window was wide open and I started to get changed just as everyone was beginning to lark around. They were in high spirits and relieved we had finally got there. When I answered an excited knock on my door, I stepped outside my room into the corridor only for the door to slam behind me, blown shut by the wind coming in through the window. I was now left standing there in the corridor in just my underpants, unable to get back into my room. As there was no lift, I had to walk down several flights of stairs in just my pants in order to get a spare key to my room then walk all the way back up again – such is life!'

Outside the hotel Peter's party of speedway fans soon encountered sinister-looking men in dark hats and black overcoats, talking in soft, secretive voices, angling to sell them the local currency, the zloty, in exchange for sterling. Much to Peter's surprise, and to some concern, they were offering twenty-five zloty to the pound, a rate of exchange that was two and a half times more favourable than what he had managed to achieve when changing currency in London. Understandably, Peter's group of fans were quick to cash in, but he was not unduly alarmed. Peter consoled himself that even if he was left with a surfeit of unused zloty at the end of the trip, he could exchange any unused notes back into sterling once more at the Polish embassy. Or so he imagined.

Happily for Peter and his party of fans, the speedway championships proved to be a huge success in every way. Just the stadium itself took the breath away. It was hugely impressive, with the 420-yard-long motorcycle speedway track surrounding a football pitch. Everyone considered the tricky journey over to Poland was worth the effort for the chance to see the current world champion Ivan Mauger, then rated as possibly the greatest rider ever, defend his world crown. Moreover, Mauger would be riding for further glory in Poland's national stadium in front of what turned out to be the largest crowd recorded in world speedway history. The stadium was hosting the world championships for the first time, and it attracted an attendance estimated at around 130,000, although reports also varied of between 90,000 and 120,000.

Best of all for the British travelling fans, the action on the track turned out to be as dramatic and thrilling a spectacle as speedway has ever produced, with Mauger and Polish rider Jerzy Szczakiel going head to head and finishing neck and neck with thirteen points each. The tie meant the two riders facing each other in a race-off in front of the massive crowd now at fever pitch. Mauger, known as the Flying Kiwi, was roared on by Peter's group of speedway fanatics who knew him well in the UK for his consistently brilliant riding with Newcastle Diamonds, Belle Vue Aces and Exeter Falcons. So there was a huge collective cry of dismay when Mauger fell on the third turn trying a risky move and the title went to the Pole. (Mauger was later to regain the world championship at the same stadium in 1979).

Despite Mauger's defeat, Peter's party were ready to drown their disappointment by hitting the large bar in the hotel, and they were in no mood to hold back. The twenty-five zloty they had traded to the pound outside the hotel went a very long way when a double vodka cost just one zloty. There were a lot of extremely inebriated speedway supporters that night, and at least fifty-seven of them were Brits.

The following day, despite the sore heads, Peter managed to get everyone back on the coach in time for the return journey to the UK, one which is remembered by all as another nightmare trip courtesy of the strict supervision by the authorities. There were frequent delays due to unreasonable and inexplicable hold-ups, unnecessary searches by menacing, grim-faced, suspicious officials and yet more checks by armed trigger-happy soldiers.

At the Polish–East Germany crossing point, border guards refused to allow anyone in the party to take any zloty currency out of the country. For

Peter, this presented a major problem: 'I now had a large unspent zloty fortune in my pocket, and I didn't want to waste it. So the only thing I could do was to spend it all, right there and then. The guards allowed just two people off our coach, so I spent an hour with John the Welder, going round every shop in town buying up crates of vodka and two dozen leather coats, and we struggled to get it all on the coach.'

For the return journey the coach party had been booked into a hotel in Cologne, West Germany, for 7 p.m., but because of all the delays they reached the hotel desperately late, at almost 7 a.m. 'We all arrived irritable and shattered with everyone whingeing and moaning and deprived of sleep. There was no time whatsoever to get our heads down. We just about had time to go into the hotel and clean our teeth before we had to set off again as we had to catch the ferry to Dover.

'I feel I aged many years through the whole experience,' Peter reflects. 'But overall it was an exceptional trip. And, again, what a great learning curve!'

* * *

While business forged ahead for Sampson Coaches and Travel Ltd, life was changing on the domestic front too. Peter was helping his mother obtain a divorce from Ben Wheatley, who had upped and vanished ten years earlier, only for them to discover that Wheatley had died three years before.

For Peter and Grace and their two small children, living with Peter's mother was not ideal. He was in essence supporting his mother and she began to seek solace from her problems in drink. 'I'd come down to breakfast in the morning and I'd have a bowl of cornflakes while she'd have a Guinness,' he says. 'She'd never go anywhere without a bottle of Guinness in her bag. I think drinking was a prop for the problems she'd had in her life and for her difficult experiences during the war. The good thing was that I never had a cross word with my mum throughout the whole of her life and, in fairness, she was always such a nice, warm, thoroughly good person.'

As Peter's mother was retiring, he was able to purchase the house from her that they were sharing and he then bought her a flat in Cheshunt, opposite the recently acquired Sampson travel agency. In time, he very reluctantly moved Gladys into an old folks home. 'I swore I'd never do that,' he says. 'But in the end, it was for the best, and she moved into a brand-new home which had been built opposite my old Riversmead school.' Peter always treated her with kindness, visited her daily and made sure she was always cared for and lacked for nothing.

Two years later, Peter and Grace decided to move with their two children to a larger house in west Cheshunt. They sold their Clarendon Road home for £13,000 and purchased, in nearby Greenbank, a new five-bed home for £28,000, which was relatively expensive at the time. Although the building of the house itself was almost fully completed, in the end the builders went out of business, leaving much to be done to the groundworks and garden. Typically, Peter chose to finish the job himself by borrowing, from Gerry Stacey, an exceptionally large JCB with a massive bucket on the front. He then had the task of driving it along the main road from Waltham Abbey to the new house in Cheshunt. 'Not easy,' he says, 'but a very interesting drive!' Within five days he had not only levelled off the land at the rear of his own house but the land of five neighbours as well, all of whom were grateful to have the size of their rear gardens increased by several feet.

* * *

Throughout the 1970s Peter's coach business flourished and expanded fast, mainly due to his acquisition of rival coach operators along with their depots, licences and contracts. This included the purchase of Eastern Enfield Coaches and Oakfield Coaches, which added six coaches to his fleet with their drivers and manager, and led to an increase in school and works contracts as well as private hire work.

The big bonus for Peter was that the council had allocated them a new site in Jeffreys Road, Brimsdown, Enfield. Over the following twelve months, he went through planning permission and built a new coach depot with one very large building which could accommodate mechanical repair workshops and body damage repairs and spraying on the other side. Downstairs provided a large drivers' room and stores and there was room enough upstairs for six offices. Grace's father Frank was in charge of the building project.

The yard area was fully concreted with lifting ramps fitted for servicing, wash bays and large underground fuel tanks. The depot could now park up to fourteen coaches and Peter admits it was only when the Brimsdown depot opened that he felt he was now a fully professional coach operator.

The next few years saw a rollercoaster of activity, firstly with the acquisition of Alexandra Coaches of Enfield and Mossrose Coaches of Waltham Abbey. The major benefits were the acquisition of their road service licences to many coastal destinations, which could help drive business, plus six more coaches as well as the drivers and their contracts.

As with Brimsdown, Peter was allocated a new site in Brooker Road, Waltham Abbey, Essex. Following his team's notable achievement in gaining planning permission, a small depot was built in less than six months with concreted yard, fences and gates, underground fuel storage, and a brick-built building with drivers' room and storage.

As business progressed, Peter secured contracts with two major nightclubs, Caesar's Palace in Luton and Blazers in Windsor. As many as three coaches set off on a Saturday evening for these venues, packed with a clubbing crowd out for a good time. Peter often drove one of the coaches himself with the clubbers given a 2 a.m. departure deadline for the return journey, in time to arrive back at the coach depot at 4 a.m. The coach would then be given a quick clean-up ready for Peter to set off again at 6 a.m., when it was still dark, to pick up anglers from various fishing clubs to take them to river destinations. 'Even in the winter they would stay by the river bank all day,' he says. 'The only way I could stay warm while waiting for their day's fishing to end was to keep walking briskly up and down inside the coach. It would be almost dusk before we set off for the journey home.'

Peter had up to five coaches regularly going out on a Sunday to various fishing locations. 'Although it seemed a good idea at the time,' he says, 'we decided to fit out part of the Welwyn Garden City shop to sell fishing tackle and equipment. But I can honestly say, it turned out not to be one of our greatest ideas.'

A much better idea was an agreement to sponsor Enfield Football FC from the 1970s into the '80s. The club was owned by Tommy Unwin, who also ran a nightclub there called the Starlight Rooms. Sponsorship included an executive coach to take the football team, the directors and the manager to away games, with the players taking the field in shirts emblazoned with the name Sampson Coaches.

One of the great benefits for Peter was an offer to attend Enfield's home matches where the extensive directors' lounge flowed with free drinks and there was an open invitation to the Starlight Rooms in the evening, where many of the big stars of the time regularly performed. 'We continued to sponsor Enfield FC for many years, during which they had a great deal of success winning trophies,' Peter says proudly. 'Now, since 2024, Hertfordshire Zoo has once again been sponsoring Enfield Town FC at their new stadium in Enfield.'

* * *

Peter is the first to admit that when he made the leap from a single school minibus contract into the coaching and travel business, it was a leap in the dark. But he threw himself into both with enthusiasm, boundless energy, a willingness to learn and an appetite for hard work allied to the ambition and drive to succeed that has come to characterise everything he turns his hand to.

CHAPTER SIX
Coast to Coast

'In the peak of the summer holiday season we had many coaches going out to a dozen of the most popular seaside destinations'

— Peter Sampson

Shortly after moving into his new house at Greenbank, Peter had the opportunity to expand his coach and travel business even further when he purchased Brunt's Coaches based in Potters Bar, Hatfield and Welwyn Garden City. The purchase included a yard, depot and shop in Potters Bar and similar in Welwyn Garden City. Grace tried to advise Peter against the purchase and he admits he should have listened. She felt it to be a step too far, but he went ahead and bought Brunt's fleet of coaches and also took on their drivers. 'What made this purchase important was that they held many road service licences (RSL),' Peter explains, 'and these licences would allow us to advertise and sell individual seats on various coach excursions and tours.

'We now had two main routes for pick-up points for our various destinations. We had our original route, which was picking up in Hoddesdon, Broxbourne, Cheshunt, Waltham Abbey, Waltham Cross and Enfield and now our new route, picking up in Welwyn Garden City, Hatfield, Potters Bar and Barnet. In the summer season, mainly from May to late September, every Saturday on both routes, we would operate coaches, mainly taking people away on holiday but also on day trips. Coaches were departing for Brighton and Worthing, Hastings and Eastbourne, Margate and Ramsgate, Clacton and Walton-on-the-Naze, Yarmouth and Lowestoft. In the peak of the holiday season, we could even have two coaches going to many of these destinations. So it became a large part of our operation and income.'

Back then, coach operators were forbidden by law to advertise coach holidays or to sell individual seats on coach excursions and tours unless they possessed an RSL. So all through the 1970s Peter invested more than £1m in buying out rival businesses, partly to acquire their RSLs. The result was that a major core of his operation in the summer season was the ability to offer holidaymakers excursions and trips away.

'At the Potters Bar depot, we had a large workshop to carry out repairs and we also had a shop to take the coach bookings,' Peter states. 'In later years, I obtained an ABTA travel agents licence for the shop, so, like Cheshunt, we could sell not only our own trips but package holidays. John Warren, the manager at the Cheshunt shop, took over at Potters Bar.

'In later years, we converted the workshop into a separate business called Shades and we had two of our team there, Derek Gleeson and Chou Maramitch, carrying out the coach conversions, fitting toilets and televisions. We also had parking facilities there for many of the coaches and likewise at the Welwyn Garden City depot as well as fuel tanks. We also added a booking office within the shop, and from these two depots, we operated school contracts and work contracts.'

As new business opportunities arose, Peter was quick to see the potential. 'We joined up with a tour company in St Albans and set up a business called Group Travellers International from our Potters Bar depot. The aim was to market school holiday trips to various destinations in the UK and Europe with us supplying the coaches. Around about the same time we set up a joint operation with Don's Coaches of Bishops Stortford called Coach Aways, marketing UK tours.

'Brian Hale, who was overseeing much of our coach work at our Brimsdown depot, came and took over at Potters Bar and Welwyn Garden City. I now realise, but not so much at the time, that renting these properties, although they did not want to sell, added to the problems in the coming years. Myself and Brian used to regularly play squash together at the club in Hoddesdon and in later years, Brian joined the team at Paradise Wildlife Park as well as overseeing part of the coach operation.'

Peter's coach business took further leaps forward when Sampsons won the contract to ferry Tesco employees to and from the supermarket's headquarters in Delamere Road, Cheshunt. The deal was first mooted after Peter was invited to a meeting at Tesco's head office regarding staff transport. Peter personally owned a small, yellow ex-BT van at the time and as he didn't think it was a great advertisement for his business he chose to park his van out of sight down the road and walk to the office. There he was greeted by Denis Baker, one of the main board directors of Tesco, who was an ex-Army officer over six feet tall with a very deep voice. 'He was an imposing figure, but in real terms a very nice person,' Peter says. Denis asked Peter to tender for a total of six coaches, one each from Bishops Stortford, Harlow, Hoddesdon, Waltham Abbey, Cuffley and one running locally. Coaches had to be at Head Office no later than 8.50 a.m. and departing in the evening at 5 p.m. After several further meetings a deal was agreed. 'It was a great contract to have,' Peter reflects. 'Bearing in mind school holidays, my school contracts were for thirty-eight weeks of the year whereas the contract with Tesco was for fifty-two weeks of the year.

'I can recall one winter evening when I was driving one of our coaches for Tesco and I was parked up in a line of our coaches outside Tesco head office in Cheshunt. It was bitterly cold so I told our drivers to keep their engines running to keep the coaches warm inside. All of a sudden Jack Cohen, the man who founded the Tesco supermarket chain, came out of the building and knocked on my coach passenger door with something to say. His exact words were: "Turn off those engines, you're wasting your governor's money using up fuel." A wise man!'

Peter made sure Sampson luxury coaches were noted for always being immaculately turned out in smart livery and carried imaginative fleet names on each side such as Sampson's King of Herts, Sampson's Adventurer and Sampson's Telstar. The Tesco contract was very special to Peter and he would often attend important meetings and occasionally provide executive coaches to take various board members to new stores around the country. He always made a point of offering his executive coaches for free as a thank-you for the work and contracts Tesco had allocated to him.

Peter remembers: 'Mr Baker was director of all transport and most things at Tesco other than food, so we would regularly meet in the autumn to discuss our contract prices for the following year. I would always say to him: "You're in charge of your transport so you know what the costs are now." Deep down, I knew he didn't and he would always say to me, "Tell me what your thoughts are." After a long debate, we would always reach an amicable agreement.'

Peter later followed up his contract to provide transport for Tesco employees by securing a further contract to provide free bus services for shoppers to and from the newly opened Tesco superstore at Brookfield Farm on the A10 at Cheshunt. The buses, specially painted in smart red-and-white Tesco livery, became a familiar sight in the Hertfordshire area. They ran hourly for shoppers from Monday to Friday to and from the store on multiple routes from Waltham Abbey and Waltham Cross, Hoddesdon and Broxbourne, Cuffley and Cheshunt.

Along with Peter's status as a successful businessman came a variety of prestigious invitations from various organisations, not least to join the Bon Accord Lodge of Masonry based at the Great Eastern Hotel in London. 'I knew nothing at all about Masonry,' he says, 'but I decided to join and as I became more involved I took more degrees in Masonry and invited several of my friends to join.' After many years of studying, he eventually became Master of the Lodge, the highest honour a lodge can bestow on its member.

On several occasions during the early 1970s Peter's coaches took groups from the local Conservative Club to various destinations, and out of the blue he was approached about the possibility of standing as a Conservative councillor for a newly formed Broxbourne Council, an amalgamation of Cheshunt Urban District Council and Hoddesdon Town Council. 'I wasn't overly keen,' he says. 'I knew very little about politics, although I was assured that I would be concerned mostly with the local environment. They convinced me to put my name forward and I was one of twenty people who were interviewed at the initial selection meeting. There I was asked, if selected, if I would be prepared to serve anywhere within the new borough. I said no, I was only interested in where I lived, which was Flamstead End, Cheshunt.

'I thought at the time my answer had got me out of being considered as a candidate, but after an hour or so I was informed I could indeed stand for election for Flamstead End but there would be two other nominated candidates in the running besides me. I felt it unlikely I would be selected but I started to go out canvassing anyway, asking people for their support. Friends warned me not to go knocking on doors at one of the housing estates as they all voted Labour, but I did so and at one block of flats a man came to his door in a grubby vest and with a pint glass of beer in his hand and his first words were: "I don't want you fiddling b******s round here." I spoke back to him in similar language, telling him in real terms that I didn't want the job of a councillor anyway. After a while he invited me in for a beer with him and when I left he said I'd convinced him that I could do a good job and that he would vote for me and ask his local friends to do the same.'

On the day of the local Borough of Broxbourne Council elections, Peter was the one chosen, finishing up with by far the most votes. 'I was uncertain as to whether I was pleased about this or not,' he says. 'But that was the start of my four-year period as a local councillor, attending meetings, sitting on the committees for planning, recreation and amenities.' In his official capacity as a councillor, Peter did his share of entertaining and was noted for his great parties and for being a generous host. This reputation led to an invitation to join the Rotary Club, where, fittingly, he was made chairman of the Entertainment and Events committee.

'Life was getting pretty difficult,' he recalls. 'I was trying to devote seven days a week to our bus and coach business, I was chairman of the Hertfordshire Coach Operators Association, and now I was involved in Masonry and I was a local councillor attending regular meetings. But becoming a member of the Rotary Club was, I felt, pretty special. Already I had friends who were members, including Brian Seaton and Harry Bishop from the Cheshunt council days and my own bank manager from the Midland Bank. So I was in good company, as they say.'

Peter's transport operation enjoyed many good years and by the late 1970s he had an impressive fleet of more than fifty coaches and buses, five depots and three travel shops. Business was booming, its success largely created by the acquisition of Road Service Licences. But buying out several coach operators' businesses came at a high financial cost.

* * *

Peter's children, Steve and Lynn, continued to be a source of great pride for Peter as they grew up. They progressed smoothly from Burleigh school to Turnford senior school. Steve moved on from joining the Cubs to becoming a Scout and then on to a Duke of Edinburgh award, while Lynn became Hertfordshire's first Queen's Guide. Both of them attended the same Dave Jones School of Dancing that Peter had attended where, interestingly, the same teachers were still there. Both Steve and Lynn fared better in the dance exams than their dad. On leaving school at sixteen Lynn took a two-year course in travel and tourism in Coventry, while Steve joined his father's coach and travel business, initially starting off in the workshops but in time going on to take and pass his coach driving test, firstly in a minibus and then a full-size coach.

* * *

Always keen to improve the services of his transport business, Peter introduced his first luxury executive coaches to include tables, table lamps, courtesy newspapers, refreshments served by hostesses on board, televisions and toilets. This up-market initiative in turn led to winning the prestigious contract with Tottenham Hotspur FC to take the football team on their travels when they were involved in European competitions. This branch of the business was overseen with great efficiency and success by Lynn, after she had successfully completed her Travel and Tourism course in Coventry. She then went on to work for Tottenham Hotspur Football Club, in their Spurs Travel Agency, and assisted in organising the European travel for the team, officials and supporters, often leading the tours by land, sea and air.

Peter's business link with speedway fans remained strong. He operated coach and bus services to meetings at Hackney stadium in east London for speedway and greyhound meetings and followed up by securing the contract to transport the Russian and Polish speedway teams on their tours of the UK. This involved removing a number of seats from two coaches in order to carry not just the riders but their bikes and various officials as well. Peter was thoughtful enough to speak to his drivers in a bid to match them with destinations which they would enjoy such as football, speedway, fishing trips or theatre outings.

Every Christmas Peter temporarily reverted to the role of coach driver himself. Many of his drivers had young children they wanted to be with at Christmas so he took it upon himself to get behind the wheel to take his family and their friends away to the coast as a festive treat. One year he drove them all in a coach to Bournemouth with his father-in-law Frank driving a packed second coach following on behind. 'There were about a hundred of us in all and we all went away together like one big family,' Grace recalls fondly. It quickly became a tradition on coastal Christmas outings for Peter, Steve and Lynn to take a swim in the sea first thing before breakfast on Boxing Day whatever the weather.

The reality for Peter of having so many vehicles on the road was that problems could occur at any moment. After a year which had not been overly successful for his business, Peter was given the shocking news in the early hours of New Year's Day that a coach on its way back from dropping passengers off at Gatwick airport had crashed on the A1 road near Hatfield, where it had careered off the road and hit a very big tree, splitting the coach in half. The impact was so great that it actually ripped off the gearbox. Thankfully the coach was carrying no passengers but when emergency services arrived on the scene, there appeared to be no sign of the driver. He was eventually discovered 60 feet away up the central reservation and was assumed to have been catapulted through his windscreen.

Miraculously, other than a few cuts and bruises the driver suffered no serious injuries. Sadly for Peter, the coach had caught fire in the crash and was a total write-off. That was doubly unfortunate as it was the best in a fleet of Brunt's Coaches which he had recently acquired.

* * *

In 1980 Peter's business took an enterprising new direction when he built and opened in Hoddesdon the first drive-through MOT testing station in the UK. He had been keen to diversify and return to how he had started out with car repairs and he set about building the MOT testing station with workshop after being granted planning permission on a site in Pindar Road, Hoddesdon.

The groundwork and foundations were nearly finished when the contracted builder went out of business, taking with him the full amount of money set aside for the project. The man Peter had employed to oversee the whole project had unfortunately already paid the full amount in advance. Peter's replacement builder, his friend Ray Chapman, declared he was unhappy with the groundworks that had been put in place and said he needed to start again from scratch. Despite these setbacks the work took less than twelve months to complete and when finished included two repair bays, stores, an office and parking facilities for clients, leaving Peter to rate Ray as 'without doubt one of the best builders and tradesmen I've ever known.' Peter named his new facility Fleetville, and it was opened in 1980 in fanfare style with the Mayor of Broxbourne cutting the ribbon.

Shrewdly, Peter designed his testing station with women very much in mind. At that time, garage workshops tended to be far from female-friendly. They were generally dirty and smelly, with posters and calendars of scantily clad girls on the walls and greasy coffee mugs on the shelves, and invariably there was nowhere for anyone to sit while waiting to collect their cars after repairs. For Peter, however, here was an opportunity to build up a good business with his MOT workshop by appealing to the growing number of female car owners and drivers. He provided customers with ladies and gents toilets and a large, clean waiting room with comfortable furniture, machines dispensing tea and coffee, and magazines and newspapers for customers to browse through while they waited.

Moreover, he made sure the waiting room had large windows so that customers waiting for their MOT could view work being carried out on their cars. This respectful approach was an unqualified success, as was Peter's personal approach in going into the waiting room after a test failure to explain to a customer why a vehicle had failed the test and then taking them into the workshop itself, the better to point out the defect in detail. More often than not, the customer would ask him to carry out the necessary repairs in his own workshop. Ernie Young, Scotty Weeks and father-in-law Frank were all now retired but helped keep the whole site clean and tidy.

Peter was also smart enough to add an extra centre lane to his testing ramp so that he could test three-wheel motors built in the style of the Robin Reliant, which became so popular through the three-wheeler van driven by David Jason as Del Boy Trotter in the hit TV series *Only Fools and Horses*. This generated a huge boost in trade as Fleetville was the only garage for many miles around with the centre lane facility. Peter believes he was also quite possibly the first garage to send out annual MOT due reminders to customers. It all helped drive the business.

Prior to opening the Fleetville facility, Peter was required to qualify officially as an MOT tester. He stayed up all night studying the rules and regulations and the following day he was pleased to see that the examiner testing him in a group of around twenty others was Bert Brown, the same man who tested his buses and coaches. As Mr Brown fired out his questions, Peter answered the first twelve straight off, prompting the examiner to remark that others must be given an opportunity to answer. But as the questions continued and no other hands were raised, Peter passed with flying colours.

To boost business and to give his fitters the day off, Peter took the opportunity to open up his MOT garage on Sundays to run Fleetville by himself for the day with the help of just a young assistant. He profited hugely from being the only MOT testing station functioning on a Sunday and, as he had the authority to train other testers, some of his existing coach fitters chose to cross over to work at the new Fleetville MOT testing station and workshop.

The success of the MOT testing station eventually led to the purchase of two coaches painted in red livery and the setting up of a company called Fleetville Coaches, which operated independently from Sampson Coaches.

As Peter's bus and coach business grew and prospered, his role in his companies inevitably changed. He emerged as a figurehead rather than as the genial hands-on operator that everybody knew and liked. 'I became more of an office worker, wearing suits and ties,' he says. 'When I'd first started the coach business I knew every customer by name. But once it had grown so big, I lost some of that close rapport I'd originally enjoyed with everyone.'

As we have seen, the Road Service Licences were vital to Peter's operation. But to his consternation, in 1980 the government, with no consultation and right out of the blue, abolished the requirement for RSLs to operate bus and coach travel. This allowed for the introduction of on-street competition for local bus services for the first time since the 1920s. 'It meant that we now had to write off a major part of our investment we'd made in buying out these other coach companies,' Peter explains.

The scrapping of RSLs meant that any coach operator, large or small, could run services on the routes which Sampsons had run independently and so successfully for several years. Suddenly Peter faced fierce competition from other transport companies offering trips to the same destinations. The long-term effect was that there were eventually too many coaches vying to pick up too few travellers, especially as passenger demand had decreased as more and more people owned cars. Gradually the whole system was grinding to a halt.

'It caused me great concern as it was a major part of our coach business income,' Peter admits. 'It was then that I started to feel that it was time to sell the coach business as I couldn't see a long-term future in it. In reality it was our contracts with Tesco and with schools that were keeping us afloat.' The sheer scale of the business was intensely challenging and all the pressure and stress eventually took its toll on Peter's marriage and he and Grace eventually parted in the early '80s, with Grace remaining in the family home with Steve and Lynn.

Entering the 1980s Peter owned an extensive coach fleet, five coach depots and three travel shops, as well as the Fleetville MOT garage. But just maintaining his position as one of the biggest independent bus and coach operators in the south of England in an increasingly competitive market was becoming more and more difficult. In some ways his business had become just too unwieldy. His fleet of vehicles required a pool of 120 drivers. Some of the buses would depart from the Essex Road depot in Hoddesdon at 5 a.m. and not return until around midnight. To comply with regulations on drivers' hours, replacement drivers were employed during the day. They weren't always easy to recruit and son Steve regularly found himself up in Newcastle and Middlesbrough trying to enlist drivers who mostly were reluctant to relocate down south.

When Steve did succeed in recruiting additional drivers, Peter found himself obliged to rent half a dozen houses in and around Hoddesdon, as well as fit them out and furnish them, in order to accommodate the new drivers, some of whom headed down south with their wives. As a goodwill welcoming gesture, Peter and Rachael would greet the new arrivals at the local station if they travelled down by train and helped them settle into their accommodation.

Sadly, the skillset as drivers among some of the new recruits often left much to be desired. There were occasions when their honesty did too. Some drivers became homesick and headed back up north again after just a few weeks and it was not uncommon for Peter to find that they had vanished overnight and taken most of the contents of the house with them, including the TV. Even knives and forks disappeared.

There were other major pressures to contend with in winter. As Peter's buses and coaches started out so early in the morning and didn't return till the small hours, the engines had to be kept running all night to prevent them from freezing up. This caused much annoyance for any neighbours who objected to all the noise.

At Peter's Essex Road bus depot, he had built himself an office in the bungalow, overlooked by the house next door, and was shocked one morning to get a telephone call from a neighbour telling him to look out of the window. On looking up he saw a man pointing a shotgun at him from an upstairs window threatening to shoot him unless the engines were turned off. Peter somehow defused the situation and appeased him by taking him round a conciliatory bottle of whisky. Peter then came up with the idea that if he rented the land at the rear of his neighbour's house, which was quite extensive, he could park many of his buses there. The outcome was that he solved the threat of being shot but it had come at great expense.

Peter eventually came to recognise that he had endured more than enough of the problems that went with operating buses and coaches. At one point he had as many as fifteen coaches travelling all over Europe and with them came huge problems when they broke down abroad; a clutch seizing up on a coach on the top of a mountain in Switzerland, a phone call telling him a head gasket had blown in Paris, another call informing him of gearbox trouble in Amsterdam, reports of a back axle breaking on a six-wheeler on one of the seven coaches he had sent off to the Belgium beer festival. These were the sort of headaches he could do without. More often than not, Peter was perfectly capable of sorting out setbacks in the UK himself, even if it meant driving many miles away at some strange hour to sort out a problem, often with his son Steve beside him. But a glitch abroad was vastly different. It meant having his breakdown truck located in France, for example, for a month at a time helping to solve the problems.

And it wasn't just the vehicles that were unreliable. As a general rule for excursions to the continent, Peter chose to book corresponding hotels for passengers himself. But one year he entrusted the hotel bookings to an agent in Belgium and fifty passengers disembarked from a Sampsons coach for a beer festival in Ostend, desperate to get some rest after a tiring journey, only to find there were no rooms at the supposedly booked hotel. The agent had disappeared with all the money. 'I had to make myself busy all around Ostend placing guests in various different hotels,' Peter recalls ruefully. Somehow he managed to find beds for the night for every single passenger.

In the second half of the 1980s, the buses Peter purchased were mainly second-hand and relatively old and they struggled to cope with an operational day that could last eighteen hours or more. Fitters did their best to maintain the buses at the workshops, working overnight, but with on-going breakdowns it was a constant challenge to keep them all in service. Any unreliability of buses mechanically meant a need either to hire alternative vehicles at extra cost or to spend heavily on new buses just to keep the services running and to fulfil contracts. The following year, the difficulties were so acute that Peter felt it necessary to order four new single-deck 70-seater buses. 'It was very expensive at the time,' he concedes, 'but we had to improve the reliability of our bus services.'

Another all too real problem to contend with was the threat of vandalism and even assaults on staff. Every bus which suffered damage from vandals would automatically be taken out of service, which in turn resulted in hiring vehicles from other transport operators. One route had to be suspended for a time after persistent vandalism by gangs of youths firing air rifles and mindlessly hurling bricks at the buses.

The huge turning point in Peter's life came in early 1984 when he purchased the old Broxbourne Zoo which stood on a large plot of land on which he was hoping to park his fleet of coaches and buses.

As we will see, Peter had no idea at the time that his purchase of land with what was widely regarded as 'the very worst zoo in Britain' would turn out to be a life-changing moment with the most seismic repercussions both personally and globally.

But for now, Peter's life was buses and coaches. 'Along with coach operators Peter Malyon and Dave Heaps I was endeavouring to work out a joint coaching programme, which in the end did not materialise. Peter and his wife Pat are still good friends of mine and Rachael's.

'We had submitted a planning application to build large new workshops to the rear of our Fleetville garage in Pindar Road. At the same time, Dave Heaps of Davian Coaches had meetings with me and it was agreed that he would purchase our coach depot, offices, and workshops in Brimsdown. This seemed the right way to move forward as we wished to relocate with much larger workshops and office accommodation in Hoddesdon, although we still had our depots in Potters Bar and Welwyn Garden City.

'At that time, Dave Heaps and his business were banking with Lloyds Bank in Hoddesdon. Since school, I had always banked with Midland Bank in Cheshunt and I'd built up a good and trusting relationship with the manager there. But Dave persuaded me to meet the manager at Lloyds Bank and at the meeting the manager had a proposal. He said he was prepared to lend Dave Heaps the money to purchase my Brimsdown site if I was prepared to move from Midland Bank and put the money I'd receive from Dave's purchase into a new account I'd open up at his Lloyds bank. He added that, if so, he'd lend me the money to build a new depot with workshops in Hoddesdon. It seemed a good idea at the time, but it proved not to be so.

'On the strength of that, and having been granted the planning permission by the Borough of Broxbourne, we started to build what was in real terms an expensive development, new yard, new workshops with all the necessary equipment and then to build a set of offices upstairs to the rear of the building.

'Confident that I had money in place with the sale of Brimsdown, contracts were signed and my good friend Ray Chapman the builder took on the work. Then, for whatever reason, still unbeknown to me, Lloyds Bank decided not to lend Davian Coaches the money. So, in many ways, I was left high and dry, which, over the coming years, caused me mega problems. I should have stayed with Midland Bank! To help out financially, I agreed to rent the depot in Brimsdown to Davian Coaches, which in a small way helped to ease the cash flow situation.

'With the hard work and dedication of Ray and the team, the new coach depot in Pindar Road was completed in less than eight months. We had all of the latest technology equipment installed for lifting vehicles, cleaning vehicles and testing vehicles, the large stores area, our own tyre depot and a good office complex. We gradually moved our fitters and members of our coach administration team from our Brimsdown depot to Hoddesdon. On paper it was a good decision as we had two large depots very close to one another and also the Fleetville garage and MOT testing station to the front of the Pindar Road site.

'Once I had completed the new workshop, which could accommodate at least six double-decker buses at a time and contained all the latest technology and testing equipment, the Department of Transport offered me the opportunity to open it as a commercial testing station for HGV vehicles. At the time,

I felt that this could be a step too far as we had to look after our own fleet, which numbered more than seventy vehicles. I turned the offer down, but in hindsight there was much more security and long-term future in running a commercial testing station than operating buses and coaches. But as I often say, hindsight is a wonderful thing.

'I eventually managed to sell the Brimsdown depot to Davian but at a greatly reduced price as that was all the money they could scrape together. We had to agree to the reduced price as Lloyds Bank were putting our business under great pressure. Sadly, several years later, Dave Heaps committed suicide.'

By the late 1980s Peter's bankers, Lloyds Bank, were extremely upset and disappointed with his external firm of accountants. 'Unbeknown to me at the time, they were eighteen months or more behind with our annual accounts,' Peter ruefully recalls. 'Looking back now, I feel Lloyds Bank themselves may have been in certain troubles or had problems with their own investments overseas.

'Suddenly I was told to attend a meeting at Lloyds Bank headquarters in London. Grace and I travelled up to town and we were invited into the office of the head of Lloyds, whose first words to me were, "We're withdrawing our services to you, and this will put you out of business due to the lack of updated accounts and information." It was a terrible shock and I endeavoured to explain that our business was still strong, that our external accountants had let me down by not producing our accounts on time, which meant I could not pass them to the bank.

'Then I said, "Hold on, I owe you all this money because you agreed to loan money to Davian Coaches, and that's the reason I changed from Midland Bank to Lloyds Bank. And then, for whatever reason I don't know, you did not loan Davian Coaches the funds to buy our Brimsdown depot. That's why we are in this financial situation we're in. It's not my fault, it's the fault of Lloyds Bank."

'The thought of the bank putting me out of business was chilling. I had given Lloyds security of our family house in Greenbank, Cheshunt, as well as the flat that I'd purchased for my mother and the house I'd purchased for

Grace's mum and dad plus our various workshops, businesses and travel shops as well as our recently acquired Broxbourne Zoo. I felt I was going to lose everything. I felt it so was unjust and, perhaps wrongly so, I expressed a few swear words and told this man I'd never met what I thought of him. It was a new lesson in life – to be careful what you give as security.

'We were then asked to leave his office and wait outside. After fifteen or so minutes, we were invited back in, and possibly my hollering and shouting had changed things a little. I was told if I could raise £50,000 in the next two weeks, they would stand by me until I had found a replacement bank.

'I was extremely fortunate that over the years I'd made some very good friends, and within three days I had raised the £50,000. Ivy Mason, who worked in our accounts office in Essex Road, part of our coach and bus department, loaned me her savings of £10,000 and numerous other good friends made up the balance.'

Once Peter had reported back to Lloyds Bank that he had raised the necessary funds, he asked Lloyds to put in writing that they would stand by him until he could find another bank. They agreed, but insisted an independent audit company, Panel Kerr Foster, visit him every month to go through the accounts of his various businesses, and Peter still had to pay £1,000 a day, a lot of money in the late 1980s – but Peter was glad to still be in business, and was looking for various ways to escape from what he felt was the difficult position the bank had put him in.

With the help of an introduction from Ron Butler of Financial Management Services, Peter and his businesses were taken on by Barclays Bank in Dartford, for which he remains eternally grateful – and a much-valued Barclays client.

'Now at least we were still in business,' Peter continues, 'but we had decisions to make as a family. Due to the financial constraints, we either had to invest more in our coach and travel business or concentrate on Broxbourne Zoo. I resolved to get out of the coaching business and dedicate all my time and energy to the zoo.

'After the reprieve by Lloyds I was looking for various ways to escape from what I felt was a very difficult position the bank had put me in. I had to implement a fresh plan to raise more funds and I decided to sell our depot in

Essex Road, Hoddesdon. My friend Tommy Unwin from Enfield Football Club offered to purchase the depot and its facilities and we agreed a price. But a few days later two gentleman arrived in smart black overcoats, carrying briefcases, to announce they wished to buy the depot. I explained to them that I had already sold it to a friend but they returned the following day asking if they could at least make an offer. I hadn't told them how much I had sold it for, but they then offered £400,000 – double the price I had already agreed with Tommy Unwin.

'It left me with a very difficult decision to make. I didn't want to let Tommy down but I was desperate for the money and realised the £400,000 they were offering would help me dispose of the buses and settle any other financial problems I had and allow me to make the final payments to Peter Phipps for the Broxbourne zoo I'd bought. So I went to Tommy and explained the situation. I told him that backing out of an agreed sale was something that I'd never done before but I felt I simply had to take the much bigger offer. In fairness to Tommy, he understood my position and generously agreed to step aside. But it was still one of the few times in my life when I didn't feel very pleased with myself. I felt bad about it.

'The good news was that I could start to sleep again. It was a great weight off my shoulders. The sale enabled me to pay off all my debts and I became debt-free. But I was foolish because what I hadn't allowed for was the tax man to come along one year later with a massive tax bill.'

In early January 1989 London Country North East agreed to buy Sampsons and the sale was concluded on 1 March. In a comprehensive review after the sale of Peter's bus and coach ventures, transport expert Ian Taylor paid tribute to the 'once proud company'. He wrote that Sampsons '... had been a household name in the area for all the right reasons a decade or so earlier. Indeed, countless Cheshunt residents must have enjoyed day trips to Clacton-on-Sea or Walton-on-the-Naze aboard a Sampson coach over the years.'

As part of the sale to London Country Buses Peter retained the minibuses and their contracts for local schools (on top of which Peter was offered a two-year paid contact to work as their advisor, which helped to fund Paradise Wildlife Park). This gave him the opportunity to set up a bus service from

Broxbourne Station to the newly acquired Broxbourne Zoo, by now renamed Paradise Wildlife Park. 'I then set up a separate company called Parkside Travel to undertake the bus service and the school contracts.

'Rightly or wrongly, I managed to get more involved with Hertfordshire County Council and school contracts, and over the course of twelve months I purchased four more large coaches, not only to carry out more contracts but private hire as well. In some ways it was additional income to help the rebuild of the zoo park.'

Since Peter had so many years of experience behind him of operating coaches, it was perhaps inevitable that once he had left the business behind to concentrate on Broxbourne Zoo, there would be attempts to lure him back. So it was no surprise when he was approached by National Express Coach Services to see if he would be prepared to tender for a luxury coach service operating from London to Edinburgh and Glasgow. The contract required a new 50-seater coach, which would have a hostess on board with tea, coffee, snacks and other refreshments, reclining seats and toilet facilities. When Peter's quotation for the work was accepted, he purchased a 50-seater Mercedes coach, which was painted white and sported the National Express livery.

'Financially it was a good contract to have,' Peter asserts, 'but the Mercedes coach didn't live up to expectations. There were various breakdown problems and I found I was driving much more myself. That's when I sat down and had a good think. I had recently sold the Sampson bus and coach business so that I could concentrate on Paradise Wildlife Park. But here I was finding myself building up a coach fleet again and getting myself more and more involved once again. Fortunately for me, I was approached by another coach operator to see if I was interested in selling the large coaches in my fleet as well as the contracts I still had and I was more than happy to do so.'

As previously, Peter was shrewd enough to retain the minibuses and their contracts while still undertaking the station runs to the park, with his good friend Alan Murphy still taking the lead. Peter then won the contract from Hertfordshire County Council for the Dial-A-Ride service. It meant he had three additional minibuses and drivers, and this carried on for several years until the contract expired. Alan continued overseeing the station run and minibus contracts up until Covid struck in early 2020, after which the operation ceased.

In truth, as we have seen, Peter had become disillusioned and disenchanted with his coach and buses business many years before he finally sold it in 1989.

'I'd invested so much time and energy in buying out other businesses to obtain their road licences that I'd made it too big to sell,' he admits. 'It was harder to get out of the business than it was to get into it, and it took me seven years to get out. Once the government had abolished road service licences and the state-owned monopoly on buses, everyone jumped on the bandwagon and everyone was chasing the same market.'

CHAPTER SEVEN
Animal Instinct
from Beasts' Belsen to Paradise

'You're buying a zoo? What do you know about animals? All you've got is a dog called Tina!'
— *John 'the Milk' Medcalf*

L ocals with long memories in the Broxbourne area can recall that the site on which Hertfordshire Zoo stands today has an association with exotic animals which dates back more than fifty years.

The wooded region was originally known as Upper White Stubbs Wood and, in 1969, a landowner by the name of Cyril Stamp submitted a proposal to the local authorities to establish a zoo in the woods. The parish council were first alerted to his plans when he chopped down a number of trees in preparation to provide enough space in which to create the small private zoo he had in mind.

The original application was turned down, but planning permission was subsequently granted on appeal in 1970, and Mr Stamp duly started up a small private zoo with chickens, goats and several other domestic and farmyard pets as well as a handful of exotic animals.

The zoo was later bought by Peter Phipps in the mid 1970s, but the bungalow and three acres of land was sold off separately to Eddie Wright and his family. Mr Phipps was essentially an entrepreneur involved in buying commercial vehicles for scrap then dismantling the engines and exporting them. But in parallel he continued to run a section of the site as Broxbourne Zoo until he largely lost interest.

When the land came up for sale in 1983, together with the zoo, it caught the attention of Peter and Grace. As we have seen, they were keen to cast an eye over the site with a view to acquiring the land for much-needed extra space on which to park their fleet of buses and coaches.

On inspection Peter deemed the land fit for purpose as a coach park, but he was also looking ahead. If he could acquire the site at an acceptable price, the freehold ownership of the land offered considerable potential for building as many as twenty houses on the premises.

So far so good. But the key condition of the sale was the insistence that the zoo must be included in the acquisition of the site.

Broxbourne Zoo at the time was by common consensus rated as the worst zoo in Britain. The poor conditions in which the animals lived and their seeming lack of care attracted placard-waving animal rights activists staging protests outside the gates on a regular basis. A 'Beasts' Belsen' was how one protester dubbed the zoo. As for Bobby the lion's enclosure, one shocked visitor declared there was barely room to swing a cat let alone allow a fully grown lion to turn around.

The sight of a chimpanzee smoking a cigarette while shackled to a garden bench on a short chain left animal lovers aghast. The conclusion for many visitors was that the zoo animals existed just for cheap entertainment without any real thoughts for animal conservation.

The mid 1980s had been tough years financially for Peter's transport business ventures, and now he had reached a stage where his confidence in his bus and coach business was fast fading. 'We had done all we could with the business,' he explains. 'We had built new depots and bought new coaches, but vehicles were depreciating too quickly, the banks were breathing down our necks all the time and we couldn't see much future in continuing. We were looking for something new, to diversify. People kept telling us to buy land. So when we came to view the Broxbourne site we were looking beyond just using it as somewhere to park our fleet of vehicles. We were looking to develop the land.'

Peter remembers that any thoughts of purchasing the land were initially met with grave misgivings by his nearest and dearest once they had seen the zoo for themselves. Son Steve described it as 'a rubbish tip with a few animals', and daughter Lynn said it 'looked like a disaster, but given time it could work out.' Peter's partner Rachael stated: 'It's the most ramshackle place, it's horrendous.'

* * *

It was while he was a local councillor for the Borough of Broxbourne that Peter had first met Rachael and she has now been his partner for forty years. They met soon after Rachael had tragically and very suddenly lost a son to illness at the age of eleven. Still grieving, Rachael had joined the local Conservatives at the time of local elections when Peter was a councillor. He had been out campaigning, and knocked on her door. He had heard of Rachael's desperately sad loss and had called on her to offer his sympathy. 'He was standing at the door with a beautiful basket of flowers for me,' Rachael remembers. 'I was quite in awe of him, and it was the first time anyone had done anything nice for me for a long time and it made me feel that someone cared. It was his way of saying that he understood my grief, that he empathised with me and wanted to help.' Rachael had a son, Andrew, and a daughter, Laura, who were both still young.

Gradually over time a friendship developed and blossomed into something more with Rachael impressed by Peter's innate kindness. 'He always was, and is, so kind,' she says. 'Peter would give you the shirt off his back. He never had anything himself, but now that he has he wants everybody else to be a part of it. He shares his good fortune and the things he has achieved. He is greatly admired by everyone who comes across him.'

After a while Peter and Rachael decided to set up home together and Peter bought a small end-of-terrace cottage in a nice location overlooking a golf course near Puckeridge in East Hertfordshire.

* * *

Rachael's reaction to Peter's purchase of Broxbourne Zoo was not unexpected. 'She was right, it was ramshackle and horrendous,' he says. 'To be fair, ninety-nine per cent of people had exactly the same opinion.' Peter already knew something of the site because he had been to a couple of car boot sales there in the past. But he had never bothered to check out the zoo because of its terrible reputation. Now he was getting his first sight of it as a potential buyer – and his opinion matched those of his family.

The opportunity to buy generated much discussion among the Sampson family. Particularly lengthy consideration was given as to what the future would hold for them all with the acquisition of the zoo being the enforced part of the deal. At the very least the zoo posed a massive challenge, and in all likelihood it would be a significant problem they could do without.

But, egged on enthusiastically by his son Steve, and with support from his daughter Lynn, Peter eventually took the decision to go ahead and buy the site, zoo and all.

Looking back, Peter says, 'I've always enjoyed a challenge and decided I'd throw myself into it. When I saw the poor state some of the animals were in, something in me wanted to make their lives better. I have to say, though, you could write what I knew about zoos on the back of a postage stamp.'

Peter reckons that at this point he was just about the only likely purchaser of the land because it had so many enforcement orders imposed upon it which deterred other potential buyers. But after negotiations, which proved to be cordial between Peter Phipps and Peter Sampson, the two men agreed on a shake of hands for the latter to purchase the 24-acre site at a price of £100,000 (around £2m in today's valuation) with a down payment and the balance to be paid off over five years.

Peter says, 'By hook or by crook I managed to scrape the deposit together and the agreement was that I would pay the balance without interest in regular monthly payments over the five years. To be fair, if the owner had been anyone other than Phippy, I wouldn't have bought the site. He was a really nice person and very easy to deal with.'

With the deal done, Phipps subsequently made a point of visiting Peter's bus and coach office in Hoddesdon each month to collect the payments.

Peter says of Phipps, 'Although there were a lot of people who didn't like him, I have to say that he was very good with me. He knew I was having trouble with the bank. He would call up and say he would drop round to collect his monthly payment and there were times when I'd sit him down, make him a cup of coffee and tell him, "Here's your coffee, but I don't have your money for you." He didn't kick up a fuss. He was very easy-going, as good as gold, told me not to worry and said he'd come back the following month. When we managed to sell part of our bus and coach business I was able to pay him in full and up to date.

'What I didn't realise when we took ownership of Broxbourne Zoo was that Peter Phipps had rented off part of the animal park to George and Betty Faye and a man called Charles. George was an established animal trainer who worked with several TV and film companies, and they stayed and worked with us for eighteen months until we agreed a financial settlement for them to move on.'

Peter's plans for building up to twenty houses on the property were soon scuppered by the local authorities. They regarded the area as part of the Hertfordshire green belt. Gaining planning permission to build would eventually prove impossible. Worse still, the local council eventually concluded that the Hertfordshire countryside was no place to park buses and coaches.

It was a major setback for Peter. 'Suddenly we were the proud owners of a site that had basically become a muddy scrapyard, a rubbish tip with a rundown shambles of a zoo with a few poorly kept in-bred animals which the local authority said was a disaster waiting to happen. We had a huge decision to make – what on earth to do with the premises we'd just bought.'

It was clear why Peter Phipps was desperate to sell. Short of money, he had invited people to dump their rubbish on the site for a fee. Just cleaning up the land would be a major challenge in itself.

Peter's plans had the full backing of Steve, then twenty-two, and Lynn, then twenty-one. 'Without hesitation they said they'd do everything to help,' he stresses. 'With them on board I knew I could make it work. It would be a steep learning curve, but the more often people told me it wouldn't work, the more I was determined to prove them wrong.'

* * *

For many years, right up until the 1980s, just about anyone in the UK could run a zoo without a licence. But increasingly there were vociferous demands from animal welfare activists for the introduction of proper legislation. They were rewarded when a Zoo Licensing Act, first proposed in 1981, finally came into force, which Peter was made aware of in late 1984!

Peter says: 'The new law required the inspection and licensing of all zoos in Great Britain. Its aim was to ensure that, where animals are kept in enclosures, they are provided with a suitable environment with an opportunity to express most normal behaviour.'

As well as improving the level of conditions and standards in wild animal husbandry, the Zoo Licensing Act additionally sought a similar improvement in visitor facilities.

Animal lovers throughout the UK rejoiced at the introduction of the act and welcomed the new regulations. The act gave them what they wanted – a law which stated clearly what constituted a zoo and laid down strict guidelines and regulations about the welfare of animals kept in captivity. It also left Peter in no doubt that the squalid conditions in which the animals existed at his newly bought Broxbourne Zoo fell a very long way short of what was now required by law. He knew the zoo would fail on multiple counts.

* * *

News of the transfer of ownership of Broxbourne Zoo quickly spread, leaving locals heaving a sigh of relief for the welfare of the animals but wondering if a bus and coach operator with no experience of animals, apart from

Peter's boyhood breeding of rabbits, could ever meet the necessary legal requirements.

The irony of Peter purchasing Broxbourne Zoo on 1 April, April Fool's Day, was not lost on the locals. They questioned Peter's dedication and commitment and considered the huge investment needed to make the zoo a viable concern was indeed a foolish venture.

Moreover, few believed Peter would ever be able to overcome the public's terrible perception of Broxbourne Zoo. Its reputation could hardly have sunk any lower. Many a visitor had gone away from the zoo and spread the word far and wide about the appalling conditions in which the animals were kept.

'No one gave us a cat in hell's chance,' Peter remembers. 'The press had a field day with us, and you can't blame them. What did we know about animals? Nothing. Nobody, but nobody, believed we would ever get a zoo licence.'

Peter was a realist, but undaunted he applied for a licence anyway, knowing that at the very least he would discover just what would be required for him to operate Broxbourne Zoo under the Zoo Licensing Act. He set up a meeting at the zoo with the licensing department of East Hertfordshire Council and a full inspection followed with officers from the local council, a ministry vet, and Molly Badham, the government-approved zoo licence inspector. Molly was the owner of Twycross Zoo and she was later to become a good friend of Peter's and a special friend of his partner Rachael.

Peter remembers: 'It was a very long and tiring day which stretched into the evening as we walked around the old Broxbourne Zoo site. We all then sat down to deliberate the very long list of what was required if we wished to have a zoo licence. The list would have filled a small book but, to be fair, it was all fully justified.'

Predictably, the inspectors informed Peter that as things stood there was no way they could grant him a zoo licence. They noted there were no fewer than twenty major conditions the zoo was failing to meet in its current state. Furthermore, there were nine immediate enforcement orders on the site. The conclusion of the inspectors was that the zoo must be shut down immediately.

It looked a hopeless undertaking for the Sampson family even to try to get the zoo up and running. But, much to the surprise of the inspectors, the family pleaded to be given at least a chance to turn the zoo around.

Impressed by Peter's determination to take up the challenge, the inspectors announced after much deliberation that they were prepared to give the family eighteen months to clean up the site, after which they would return to ascertain if it met all the legal requirements sufficiently enough to re-open as a zoo. 'We were under no illusions,' Peter says. 'It was a tough eighteen-month deadline but at least we now knew exactly where we stood.'

To comply with the orders of the government inspectors, Peter duly closed down Broxbourne Zoo on Christmas Day 1984, ceasing operations immediately. Finding homes for the collection of domestic and farmyard animals proved none too difficult, but the more exotic animals, including two camels, pumas, two aged wolves, macaques, squirrel monkeys, apes and Bobby the lion, were a different proposition.

Sadly, the two wolves turned out to be so old and frail and in such poor health that they had to be put to sleep, as did one of the pumas after it had suffered a stroke. But the Sampson family were at pains to ensure the remainder were suitably rehomed with other zoos or animal sanctuaries. The exception were four llamas, two Vietnamese pigs, which they kept, and Bobby the lion, whom Peter instinctively chose to retain. He had developed an affection for the lion right from the start and felt a sense of duty to address his pitiful plight.

Faced with a long list of rigorous challenges akin to the twelve great labours of Hercules, the Sampson family set about meeting them one by one. But with the full agreement of everyone, Peter was adamant that the first task had to be the building of a new enclosure and house for Bobby the lion. As we have seen, that was the family's top priority.

With zero knowledge of how to care for and keep a lion, Peter wisely decided to retain the services of Yvonne Cullum, the girl who had been looking after Bobby at the zoo for several years. She had not been paid for months.

Yvonne had been working as a negative cutter at a film library when she arrived at Broxbourne Zoo as a visitor one day in 1976 and quickly decided to become a volunteer at the zoo at weekends. 'I saw that the cages were awful,' she says, 'and I wanted to make a difference.' But with the zoo now under the ownership of the Sampson family, Yvonne knew major changes were likely and feared that her services as Bobby's keeper might no longer be required. But to her delight she found it was the reverse. She quickly became an integral part of Peter's team.

'Peter was wonderfully welcoming,' Yvonne remembers. 'He said that I came with the zoo he'd bought and that he wanted me to stay. He knew I wasn't being paid for looking after Bobby, and he immediately sorted out some regular wages for me. He also agreed to pay for fuel for my car to travel to and from the zoo and to and from the slaughterhouse to get meat.

'I was so excited about the zoo getting a new owner. There were all those years when no one had cared and I had no money to do anything about it. But I could see Peter really cared. The previous owner had his heart in the right place and had tried his hardest but the money wasn't there to improve things. Conditions were getting worse and worse and there were an increasing number of protestors campaigning for the zoo to be closed down.

'Poor Bobby the lion was not in good shape. He had developed sores on his paws from constantly pacing up and down on the concrete floor of his small cage. In an effort to ease the pain I laid straw down all over the concrete and a vet gave me cream for his feet. Bobby would lie down and I'd reach through the bars of his cage to rub the cream on to his paws.'

At one point prior to Peter's takeover of the zoo, animal activists must have decided Bobby was in such a bad way that the kindest thing would be to put him out of his misery. One night the zoo suffered a break-in and Bobby, along with several of the other animals, was fed chicken laced with poison. All of them became ill, and Bobby severely so.

'I thought we were going to lose him,' says Yvonne. 'I discovered him off his legs slumped down in his cage. No big animal can lie down in the same position for lengthy periods, so we had to turn him over and massage him all over his body and place straw bales all around him to stabilise him. Bobby became desperately thin, and I began feeding him small bits of meat by hand and the vet gave him something intravenously to keep him hydrated.

'Bobby struggled on until one day I was cleaning out his cage and I suddenly felt him leaning up against me. Without my knowing he had even got himself to his feet. I had this amazing warm feeling that such a big animal had come up to me with affection like that, and I stroked him. Thereafter I went into Bobby's cage once a week to feed him until he got his strength back. From then on we had a bond. Bobby was my everything. It was so humbling to have such a great relationship with such a big beast.'

Having secured Yvonne's future as Bobby's keeper, Peter began work with advice from other zoos to build the new fit-for-purpose enclosure for the lion which he had promised.

Just as it was for Peter, so it was also a very special moment for Yvonne to savour when Bobby was rehomed. She had lavished so much love and care on Bobby, in particular on his painful paws, and now those paws were joyfully padding around on soft grass. 'When he first came out into the enclosure, he looked up at the sky in wonder,' Yvonne says. 'In his previous cage he couldn't even see the sky.'

By rehoming the lion on site, Peter most certainly prolonged Bobby's life by many years. But it was not just an act of compassion; it was a pivotal moment too in the history of Paradise Wildlife Park and an impressive statement of intent.

Extraordinary to relate, and Bobby would have known nothing of it, but Peter went on to save the lion's life twice more. Shortly after his initial purchase of the zoo, and with Bobby now comfortably rehomed, Peter was stunned by the sudden arrival at the site of a complete stranger, a woman, who blithely declared, 'I've come to collect my lion.'

It turned out the woman was under the firm impression that Bobby was hers. She claimed that Bobby had been leased out to her by a previous owner. There may have been a small vestige of validity in her claim but there was no documentation, no concrete proof. Peter, however, was determined Bobby was going nowhere and decided that even though he had in effect paid for Bobby once already, he would find the money to settle the matter of ownership. 'Incredibly,' Peter says, 'a fortnight later another woman, again a complete stranger, turned up to tell me that she too had come for her lion. I couldn't believe it.'

It transpired that some underhand double and triple dealing had been afoot long before Peter's purchase of the zoo. But having set his mind on keeping Bobby, Peter solved the issue by paying up once again. Given his financial constrictions at the time, it was a generous gesture and once again an admirable statement of intent. It ensured Bobby would live out his days properly fed and cared for, the very first of the animals of Broxbourne Zoo to benefit from larger enclosures.

Peter and his family had the added pleasure of watching Bobby's relationship with Yvonne blossom and flourish with mutual warmth and affection. Once rehomed, Bobby took on a new lease of life under her care and formed such a loving affinity with her that he came to recognise the noise of her VW Beetle's engine every time she drove into the park.

'It was uncanny. He would listen out for her and he recognised the sound of her car so well as soon as he heard it,' Peter says. 'He'd lift his head, prick up his ears, rise to his feet and pace expectantly up and down ready to greet Yvonne. And I'm pleased to say that Bobby went on to live comfortably at Paradise Wildlife Park to the end of his life. Bobby died at the age of eighteen, so when you take into account that lions average around ten years of life in the wild, then eighteen was a very good age considering how he had spent the first few years of his life.'

In time, Yvonne left Paradise, got married and moved away to live in Cornwall. But when it became clear to Peter that Bobby was nearing the end of his life, he telephoned Yvonne to inform her that her beloved lion's days were numbered. Bobby's life was slipping away, and Peter thoughtfully asked whether she might wish to be with him at the end. It was a measure of Yvonne's love and affection for Bobby that she immediately made arrangements to drive up to Broxbourne from her home in Cornwall to be with him for the last time.

Old and weak as he was, Bobby responded once more to the sound of Yvonne and he rallied enough for the two of them to have the most poignant of reunions. For two days Yvonne was able to make a fuss of him until he died in her arms. 'I went into his enclosure and sat with him for the last time,' she says. 'I was the only one who could have done that, and he had his head on my lap when the vet put a needle into his vein.' Yvonne was deeply saddened as Bobby slipped away and her grief was shared by everyone at Paradise Wildlife Park.

CHAPTER EIGHT
Welcome to Paradise

'This will be an asset to the community'
— *Councillor Peter Sivyer*

Before Peter could even think of creating a zoo from scratch, a huge clean-up operation was required for the entire Broxbourne site. Quite apart from numerous pot holes and layers of mud to contend with, the site was a mixture of a breaker's yard, a scrap heap, a building site, a communal rubbish tip, a fly-tipping dumping ground and a place to burn waste materials.

To turn the zoo around would require massive investment as well as dedicated hard work, and all the while Peter had a bus and coach business and a travel shop to run, as well as the MOT testing station.

The site's primitive buildings, dilapidated tin sheds and unsafe animal cages needed to be pulled down, repaired or renovated, and among the rubbish and rubble to be removed were hundreds of old tyres, broken bricks, planks of wood, scrap metal and slabs of concrete.

More worryingly, the land needed to be levelled and there was no mains water supply, no gas, barely any electricity, no drainage, one old lavatory and a cesspit.

The water issue was a particular problem. The sole source of water came from an ancient 30-foot-high storage tank at the top of a water tower. The problem for the Sampson family was that it was set on three acres of land still in the ownership of their neighbour, Eddie Wright. He used the water not just for his own bungalow but for a nearby neighbour along with the zoo, and since Peter required the same water source for his own projects, it was bound to cause friction and so it eventually proved.

It became apparent from the start that the water tower was barely fit for purpose. It was without doubt far from hygienic, and difficult to maintain. In winter the ball valve was prone to freeze up completely and Health and Safety officers today would have had a fit if they had witnessed Peter clamber up two ladders precariously tied together with rope to enable him to reach the top of the tower to inspect the storage tank. Lifting the huge, ill-fitting, heavy lid and peering into the tank, Peter found dead pigeons and squirrels and other detritus snarling up the supply. It all made for a difficult working relationship with Mr Wright.

Eventually, as funds allowed, Peter installed a ground-level reservoir tank which held 20 cubic litres of water. It was, and still is, fed by a pumping and filtering system over 200 feet below ground. In the following years Peter added two more ground-level water storage tanks with pumps to push the water around the site. With the help of builder Ray Chapman the high water tank tower was dismantled.

The schedule of works would eventually include animal enclosures and houses, fencing and paddock buildings, public facilities, improvements to pathways and tree planting. But it was the infrastructure which required the most urgent attention – the water supply, improved electricity supply and a sewage treatment system.

While Peter was predominantly still involved in running the coach business, an initial team to tackle the site comprised Peter's two children Steve and Lynn, their good friend Tim Harrison, another friend by the name of Mark Harris and a woman called Chris Evans who handled the secretarial work.

From when the zoo was purchased in 1984, Steve, Tim and Mark all lived in an old caravan on site with a rescued terrier called Sally. They also found room in the caravan to take in a recently born crab-eating macaque, Charlie, whom they took pity on after he had sadly been rejected by his mother. It was hardly five-star luxury living for the lads. After a twelve-hour day spent toiling away doing the dirtiest of tiring work, it was inevitable that some of the dirt would infiltrate the caravan. 'It was a hellhole,' says Steve bluntly, but with a chuckle. 'My dad used to say it was the only place he'd ever been in where you had to wipe your feet on the way out!'

Part of the problem was Charlie the monkey, who proved full of mischief, especially at mealtimes. Charlie was prone to swiping food off the team's plates while they were enjoying a hard-earned bite. He was well cared for and well fed, but cheeky Charlie would make a grab for anything the team were tucking into, especially curries. Slyly, he also slugged back beer from their glasses when the boys weren't looking, with predictable results.

One evening, after a hard day's toil, the boys were sitting back watching television when Charlie suddenly toppled off the sofa, having secretly helped himself to too much homebrew. Worse was to come. When it came to hygiene, Charlie's habits left a great deal to be desired. He was full of fun but his popularity slipped several notches on the night he relieved himself while perched on top of the television set, causing the TV to blow up while the lads were watching football!

Sally, the rescue dog, took it upon herself to foster Charlie and as the baby monkey grew the warm relationship between the two animals provided much amusement for the hard-working team as well as companionship at the end of a tiring day. The animal duo's pièce de résistance was Charlie taking a ride on Sally's back. The sight of Sally running around the site with Charlie cheerfully clinging on like a jockey never failed to amuse, especially as both animals clearly enjoyed it.

Steve Sampson was given the task of tackling the urgent renovations. He says: 'Almost everything we did during that first year was under the ground: putting in drains, setting up the water supply and electricity, and a planned on-site restaurant from an existing café building had to be underpinned. That first year was taken up with tough, really hard manual jobs. People would come up to see how we were getting on and they'd say, "You haven't done much, have you?" That was because nearly all the work we were doing was under the ground and you couldn't see the hard work we'd put in.

'For the best part of that first year, every day was exactly the same. It was work, pub, leave! That was our life, and the only day we could tell it was Sunday was when the pubs closed early.'

Frustratingly for Steve and his on-site team, Peter had the uncanny knack of arriving to check on their progress just when they all happened to be taking a well-earned break. It looked to him for all the world like they were slacking on the job. 'It became a standing joke,' Steve says. 'We were really grafting hard, but I can guarantee that whatever time of day we happened to stop for a coffee or a sandwich, that was the exact time my dad would arrive. All he'd ever see was us taking a break.'

In the zoo's early days Peter rolled up his sleeves himself and joined the workforce whenever time permitted. His welding skills, especially, came to the fore. Until he built his own large workshop, he drove around the park in a large high-top transit van converted into a mobile workshop containing all his tools and welding equipment. On Saturdays he'd spend a full day at the site building and welding, and many an evening too.

Family, friends and employees from Peter's coach business also joined in, swept along by Peter's customary zest and energy and his determination to get a job done, and done well. Gradually Sally became Peter's dog and a loyal pet, spending all day by his side, following him everywhere as he busied himself around the park.

To help with the running costs of Paradise, Peter agreed to a proposal by Dave and Henrietta Manning to rent an area of the site for fairground rides and a small cabin food bar. The rental money was a welcome help to Peter and the couple stayed for over twenty years. To create more funds for development, two cabins were rented out, one to an electrical business and another to a company which operated tipper lorries. Space was also found for the building of a car pound for ECP Motors to park up new Ford cars, and further space was allocated to Arlington Coach Sales to park up a few coaches. The rental Peter received was hugely beneficial, but this much-needed source of income was brought to a halt by the local authority, who decided rentals involving tipper lorries, coaches and cars were inappropriate for a designated green belt. It had been good while it lasted.

It took eighteen months of relentless toil with improvements carried out in line with experts' recommendations before Peter was ready to face the scheduled visit from the zoo licence inspectors. By the time they arrived the only animals in residence were Bobby the lion, four llamas and two Vietnamese pigs.

The inspectors were astonished at what they saw. They were impressed at how much had been achieved in such a relatively short space of time. They confessed that as they had walked away after their original inspection they hadn't given the family the remotest chance of meeting their demands. Now they could see that all the hard work of the Sampson family had paid off, and crucially East Hertfordshire District Council were prepared to grant Peter a zoo licence enabling him to re-open the site officially at Easter 1986.

East Hertfordshire Licensing Officer Peter Sivyer was particularly impressed by the change in Bobby the lion's circumstances: 'A new lion enclosure has recently been completed giving conditions which are rated by one of the inspecting veterinary surgeons as excellent,' he told the local press. 'An existing building has been totally refurbished to give a food preparation area with steel-lined storage bins, an area for veterinary care and staff rest room.'

No expense had been spared, he enthused, and the whole area of the zoo was enclosed by a perimeter fence separating it from the rest of the park. He noted with evident approval that a certain amount of in-house training had taken place with the help of a consultant vet and that three members of staff were to attend a special course in Cambridge for people working with zoo animals.

Peter had wisely called in experts at all stages of the redevelopment of the zoo. Prudently he had also invited an inspector to visit on behalf of the council on several occasions as work progressed. It meant the inspector could oversee that everything was being done correctly. It prompted Councillor Eric Marshall to describe the transformation as 'quite remarkable', while Councillor Bob Perrett was moved to say there was no comparison between the 'festering sore' the zoo had been for some time and the 'fine complex' it was now.

In a glowing summary, Mr Sivyer said, 'The owner has always stated that it was his intention to provide an area for the family to be able to spend a pleasant time surrounded by countryside and a small animal area. This has been achieved and will be an asset to the community.'

The Sampson family sensibly chose to open the zoo under a new name in order to distance themselves from the appalling reputation earned previously by Broxbourne Zoo. Originally they proposed to call it Paradise Park, but there were objections and the threat of legal action from a zoo in Cornwall with the same name. The new name of Paradise Park and Woodland Zoo reflected the lean towards environmental education and open enclosures for the animals.

Understandably, however, the re-opening was greeted with scepticism by some of the local community. They questioned whether the Sampson family knew what they were doing. The family were known for running a transport company with a fleet of coaches and buses and had no experience of life caring for big animals. They doubted the family could make a success of it.

John 'the Milk' was just one of many of Peter's friends who wished him well but believed he had taken leave of his senses in buying the zoo.

It would take years before the Sampson family would become totally accepted within the zoo fraternity. 'To begin with, no one in the zoo world would entertain us,' Peter says. 'They regarded us as just a load of mavericks who didn't know what we were doing or what we were talking about. To be fair we had very little knowledge. But, as I often say, life is a learning curve. As we gradually got to know people, they saw that we were enthusiastic about what we were trying to do and they warmed to us.'

* * *

Now that Bobby the lion was enjoying life in his new enclosure, Peter's next main task was to rebuild what had been the old café building at Broxbourne Zoo. With income from Paradise nowhere near covering the expenditure, he stripped the café down, created a new building and turned it into a restaurant with brand-new kitchens. Much of the work was carried out by Peter's cousin Terry Keates and Terry's father, who had started up their own building company.

Once the project had been completed, Lynn gave up her job at Tottenham Hotspur FC's travel operation to manage the catering side of the park, and a year later she set up her own company, Pembridge Banqueting Ltd, which over time proved to be very successful. The added benefit for the park was Lynn paying a rent on the business, which helped towards the costs of some of Paradise's improvements and development.

Lynn was helped out in this catering venture by Craig Whitnall, an Australian who was on a rugby tour in 1989 and found himself in the UK with friends all looking for some work over Christmas before travelling to Africa. He approached her for work, and settled in very quickly. With Craig's help the business soon expanded into being very much more than just a day-to-day cafeteria. There were weddings to cater for on Saturdays, as well as many other events and functions, including children's parties, and Sunday lunches became famous for the restaurant's home-cooked carvery.

On Thursday and Friday nights Lynn and Craig ran the restaurant together as a nightclub, The Zu Club, with a disco, with brother Steve as the DJ. They also brought in live bands, including a local Sixties group called The Overtures who became regular favourites with the clubbers. After a slow start, attendance grew in a matter of weeks from around twenty to thirty people to more than five hundred.

'My job was to stand at the bar and get people up to dance,' says Peter, who was always loyally supportive of Lynn running the nightclub.

'It didn't matter what sort of event or function we were hosting,' Lynn says, 'he would always be there from the start. He would be first on to the dance floor, helping to drag everyone up. He'd get the whole evening going no matter if there were ten people there or two hundred. He's still the same – he makes everyone join in, gets them going, having a good time.'

Lynn and Craig made a great team, and everyone was delighted when romance blossomed between the hard-working couple and they got married on 13 April 1991.

The only hiccup about running the restaurant as a nightclub was the threat of the water supply being switched off. Inevitably the atmosphere became livelier as the evenings wore on and Eddie Wright had the power to stop the water if his demands for the noise to be turned down were not met. After much negotiation and some ill feeling that they were partly being held to ransom, Lynn and Craig decided the only solution was for them to purchase Eddie Wright's land and with it the bungalow called Wood House which stood on it. It proved to be a wise move, and over time Lynn and Craig cleared the land of scrap and old enclosures and refurbished the house with Ray Chapman.

The Pembridge operation quickly became a 24/7 venture. To help with additional Paradise building costs, the park rented part of the land from Lynn and Craig and built a Birds of Paradise area with high aviaries containing a collection of various birds including parrots, birds of prey and owls. Peter also built a seated area for free-flying bird displays as well as an under-cover aviary for lorikeets.

* * *

As Peter began to devote more of his time to creating Paradise Wildlife Park, he decided to sell his Fleetville garage and MOT testing station in Hoddesdon. He had many regrets, but by retaining the property itself he received a rental income which went towards Paradise funding. Shrewdly, when he had sold his coach business to Arriva, Peter had also taken up the company's offer of a two-year consultancy contract. 'These additional funds were most useful in investing in the development of Paradise,' he says.

CHAPTER NINE
A Rocky Road to Tiger Love

'Rocky was the most sweet-natured tiger. He never showed any aggression. At two years old and fully grown he was still sucking my thumb'

— *Peter Sampson*

The first tiger to arrive at Paradise was Padmini, a Bengal tigress. Steve and a colleague, Barry Bright, travelled to the Isle of Wight Zoo at Sandown on Christmas Eve 1992 to collect Padmini, then a nervous six-month-old cub being hand-reared by the zoo's owner Jack Corney. At Paradise, Padmini continued to be hand-reared by Steve's wife Angela, who patiently spent up to four hours a day sitting with the young tigress throughout a freezing winter until Padmini would fall asleep with her head resting in Angela's lap.

Angela played a major role in raising Padmini, and as time went by she developed a remarkable relationship with the tigress. She was eventually able to fit a collar on Padmini so she could walk her around the park. Inevitably Angela was regularly stopped on her rounds by Paradise visitors eager to have a photograph taken with the tiger. This in turn led to Angela coming up with the idea of pioneering a scheme whereby visitors could pay for the privilege of posing with the tigress for photographs in order to help raise money to build Padmini a larger enclosure.

Steve gives full credit to Angela for initiating the animal experience programme at Paradise. 'Angela led the way and we then became the first zoo in the country to introduce a Shadow A Keeper scheme. We were the leading zoo in Europe offering these kinds of animal experiences.

'Acquiring Padmini from the Isle of Wight Zoo, combined with our ability to have Paradise Wildlife Park featured on television, transformed the whole business for us. The years from 1994 to 1996 were remarkable. We were on TV around two hundred times in two years, including twenty-six weeks on the Nickelodeon Channel. We were also regularly featured on *The Big Breakfast* with presenters Chris Evans and Gaby Roslin, all of which made a terrific difference in terms of general awareness of the park.'

* * *

The acquisition of animals for Paradise was never going to be straightforward. 'At first we tried to talk to other zoos, but they were wary and suspicious of us,' Peter says.

'It took us ten years to be fully accepted by the zoo fraternity, and for a long time now we've been highly respected in the industry. But in the beginning just about the only people who showed any interest in us were circus folk. So from the first days of Paradise Wildlife Park we worked with friends and people from the circus world.'

Prior to the passing of a law in January 2020 banning wild animals from performing in circuses in the UK, it was relatively common for a circus to include an act involving lions or tigers. As such, Peter soon found a friend in Martin Lacey, a well-known trainer of lions and tigers and founder of The Great British Circus, a UK-based company specialising in circus entertainment.

Martin had a circus which at the time ventured far and wide, and if a tiger cub was born while the circus was on the move it was difficult for the circus folk to rear it. Thus it suited both Martin and Peter if the latter was prepared to travel quickly to wherever the circus was currently located to pick up the cub and give it a home.

'When circus tigers and lions gave birth we were only too happy to take their cubs into our care, bottle-feed them and rear them,' Peter says. 'I don't like hand-rearing, but I can't just let tiny cubs lie there and die. I have to give the animal a chance.'

One evening Peter received a call from Martin Lacey in Newcastle offering him a tiger cub just a few days old. Peter needed no second invitation and accompanied by Rachael he drove through the night to reach Newcastle the following morning, a journey which brought back memories of his days when he rode at Newcastle speedway.

That morning Peter and Rachael collected a very small tiger cub weighing just 2 lbs, and on the journey back south they stopped every two hours to bottle-feed the cub, which they named Bruno. 'We continued to hand-rear the cub over the coming months,' Peter says proudly, 'and I am pleased to say Bruno grew to be a splendid tiger and eventually fathered a cub of his own.'

In addition to his working relationship with Martin Lacey, Peter soon struck up a similarly good connection with Tommy Chipperfield, animal trainer at Tom Duffy's circus in Ireland. He understood that Peter was trying to build up the number of animals at Paradise and he got in touch whenever a tiger or lion cub was born and then rejected by the mother. It resulted in Peter personally making several journeys across to Ireland during the early years of Paradise to collect newly born cubs.

Peter recalls: 'One of the first journeys we made was by van and ferry to collect two young tiger cubs. Giles Clark, my apprentice at the time, who was to go on to play a major role at Paradise, and eventually at The Big Cat Sanctuary too, was not old enough at that point to hold a driving licence so I had to do all the driving. What with the meetings and ferry journeys back and forth, it took us just over three days with me getting barely a wink of sleep.

'As the two young tiger cubs started to grow, Giles took a leading role in the raising of them and it was then that I knew that this was the start of a long and great adventure for me and Giles into the world of tigers and conservation.

'During the mid 1980s, through the 1990s and even into the start of the 2000s, friends from the circus world advised and worked with us with various animals. We had what I felt was a great relationship with circus folk, including circus animal trainer Jim Clubb. Sadly, it came to an end only because, as we gradually became members of the various zoo associations, it was frowned upon for us to work with circuses.'

Looking back Peter asks himself, 'Did I like circuses? Not really. The lions and tigers were in the wrong environment. Did I like the people who looked after circus animals? Yes, I did. Circus people generally looked after their animals exceptionally well.'

＊＊

Launching Paradise was a sharp learning curve for Peter and full of surprises. Everyone knows that wild animals can be unpredictable in their behaviour and none more so than the llama which mystifyingly chose in the early days of Paradise to make an unscheduled dash for the nearby woods. The llama had lived very happily and safely at Paradise for many months behind a six-foot fence specially built to house it, when for no apparent reason it suddenly jumped over the fence on to the driveway and took off.

'It was free for two weeks,' Peter remembers. 'I was frightened all the while it was free that it would perhaps run in front of a motorbike or a car and cause an accident in which someone would be killed. So, very reluctantly I decided I had to bring in a marksman.

'We contacted him on a Monday but he said he couldn't come the following day but would arrive on the Wednesday. Then to our amazement, not to mention our relief and joy, the llama calmly walked back in through the main gate, trotted down the drive and jumped back into its enclosure again just as suddenly as it had left.'

Peter has never been fond of guns and firearms. But part of his zoo licence required him to be able to fire a gun in an emergency and he underwent many days of training at the Bisley shooting range in Surrey and emerged legally able and qualified to fire a gun.

Peter was conscious from day one that safety was paramount and in the early days there were one or two nervy moments at Paradise when he walked the tigers around the park. Weighing close to thirty-five stone, a tiger might suddenly decide it was time for a rest and choose to sit down in the car park just when it was getting near to the park's opening time. Persuading a big cat to get a move on when it wanted to take it easy was no simple task and Peter, with help from members of his team, would be forced to tempt the animal to shift with pieces of chicken.

The park had a three-gate system to ensure no animal could get out. 'But four camels somehow did manage to escape and went running up the country lane,' he recalls. 'We had motorists phoning up the police to say there were camels on the loose. However, we managed to marshal them up the drive of a nearby cottage, where we were able to secure them and bring them back to Paradise.'

As with the llama, Peter can reflect on the incident with relief and some amusement. 'You can leave university with all sorts of qualifications and degrees,' he says, 'but it doesn't teach you how to chase a camel up an English country lane!'

* * *

There is an old adage in showbusiness that says if you are making a film, a television programme or putting on a live show, never work with children or animals. Peter did both, and the adage proved to have something of a general truth about it on a famous occasion during the early days of Paradise Wildlife Park.

Peter's son Steve, who was planning and organising events around the park, arranged for two camels to be transported all the way into the Sussex countryside for a children's birthday party. The immediate problem was how to convey the animals from Broxbourne to the outer fringes of Eastbourne. The solution was hiring a large lorry-horsebox, old and not in the best shape, and with it the realisation quickly dawned on Peter that he would be the one who would have to drive it. 'I'd drawn the short straw,' he says. 'I was the only one among us all who possessed an HGV licence qualifying me to drive it. Only I could get behind the wheel for the long, slow journey.'

It took the best part of an hour of pushing and shoving before the camels were finally coaxed into the lorry and Peter, accompanied by Rachael, was able to set off.

On the way he needed to stop at a petrol station to refuel and the camels caused a commotion by choosing that pause in the journey to relieve themselves while the vehicle was parked at the petrol pump. The resulting tsunami which flooded across the garage forecourt caused another motorist to believe that one of the petrol pumps had sprung a leak and he rushed off to find the petrol station manager to raise the alarm, leaving Peter and Rachael to make a hasty departure.

As instructed by the party hosts, Peter and Rachael arrived in Sussex at the top of a country lane a quarter of a mile from their destination. There they were met by their hosts with a special request: in a bid to authenticate their visit with the camels, they were asked to dress up in Arab-style costume. It seemed a not-unreasonable request and one they could hardly refuse when the hosts produced appropriate costumes – a pair of silk pyjamas for Peter to wear with a towel to wrap around his head as a turban, and for Rachael an ill-fitting garment she remembers as being at least two sizes too small.

The next problem was how to entice the camels out of the horsebox. They were as reluctant to come out as they had been disinclined to go in. It took half an hour until the 'ships of the desert' decided it was time to emerge from the horsebox.

Much to the astonishment of passing motorists, the camels were led by a head collar and lead for a quarter of a mile up a country lane into a paddock area, where their arrival was greeted with understandable squeals of excitement by the young birthday party guests. Then came the inevitable question from the hosts: 'Can the children have a camel ride?'

Taking up the story, Rachael says: 'That wasn't going to be easy because the camels had never had anyone sit on their backs before. We eventually did manage to get them to sit down and take children on to their backs, but when they stood up again, they wouldn't move.'

Camels can be stubborn creatures, and these particular ships of the desert refused to budge. 'In the end we managed to acquire a bucket of apples and walked in front of them with the reins in one hand and the apples in the other as bait to get them moving. We carried on for several more hours like this with the apples as enticement. But by the time the camels had carried out many rounds of the paddocks they had eaten the entire bucket of apples, were a little intoxicated and started to stagger.' As every cider company will testify, apple juice can turn potently to cider.

It was time to give the camels a rest and a break, and the animals were securely tethered to a large stake in the ground, which allowed Peter and Rachael to head off for a coffee. 'But all of a sudden the camels took off,' Rachael continues. 'Somehow they managed to pull up the stake to which they were tied and raced off with a long steel stake swinging from side to side.'

The camels were eventually retrieved and calmed down with no harm done either to Peter or Rachael nor to any of the birthday party guests. 'They all thought it was wonderful,' says Rachael, 'the most fantastic day of their lives! It was certainly a different day for us, chasing after two runaway camels while all dressed up looking like rejects from *Lawrence of Arabia*!'

It was starting to get late in the day by the time Peter and Rachael were able to bid farewell to all the children and start leading the camels on the slow quarter-of-a-mile walk back to the lorry-horsebox for the even slower drive back to Broxbourne. On return Peter and Rachael reflected that they had probably had far better days.

***

Over the coming years as PWP's reputation grew impressively, planning permission was gained to build a large complex that Peter called Tiger Lodge, which consisted of a big double-sided central house with two extremely large, landscaped enclosures. Peter himself took on the steel work, welding and fencing and the project was completed within six months.

Keeping pace with all the restructuring, animals arrived at the park from a wide range of locations. Keen to add different species, Peter bought a Brazilian tapir from Port Lympne Safari Park in Kent and a plains zebra from West Midland Safari Park at Bewdley in Worcestershire which helped increase the number of paddock animals.

* * *

During the first few years of Paradise Peter had made many journeys by road over to Ireland to collect lion and tiger cubs born into circuses. But increasingly he preferred to go by light aircraft. It was far less stressful than three very long and tiring, largely sleepless days behind the wheel of a van.

He says: 'I took to chartering a very small plane from Panshanger, an extremely basic airfield near Welwyn Garden City, approximately 10 miles from the park. It had previously been used by the RAF for training purposes and it consisted of just a large grass field and a timber shed. For our first flight we were required to be at the airfield in the early hours. I was itching for us to take off as soon as possible but we sat there drinking endless cups of coffee. When I asked the pilot why we were waiting so long to leave he explained that the field and runway had no lights, and he was waiting for daylight as otherwise he wouldn't be able to see where he was going.

'Once airborne, I soon realised that drinking so many cups of coffee while we had waited was not a great idea. There was no loo onboard this small biplane. On one occasion we were in the air bursting to relieve ourselves and the pilot had to put out a mayday request for us to land in Dublin next to the big jets so we could rush to the loo as soon as we landed.'

The flights to Ireland were rarely straightforward. 'On the way we sometimes had to land first at a small grass airfield, again a very basic strip, in north Wales for customs clearance. Again it was all very primitive with just a shed with a telephone attached on one side of it and there we had to dial up the customs officer, who would turn up on his bicycle to sign our paperwork. Only then were we ready to fly on to Dublin.

'On one occasion I was flown over to Ireland by a newly qualified young pilot who, to my alarm, told me once we were up in the air that he was uncertain of the route to follow once we had crossed the Irish Sea. He took to flying extremely low so that he could follow the motorway direction signs to Dublin.'

Time was of the essence on every trip. A quick turnaround was required. 'After landing in Dublin the pilot would park up and wait to fly us back. The pick-up from Tommy Chipperfield was a 20-mile taxi ride away and it was always a hasty collect and return, knowing that we had the light aircraft and the pilot waiting for us.

'On the way back I would always aim to hurry through customs with the young cub in a small carrying case. I was always trying not to be noticed and I generally managed to get through without any undue attention except for one occasion when a customs official, a woman, looked up and asked to see what was in my carry case. I told her I had a small cat and she asked to see it. So I placed the carrying box on the counter and opened the hatch, expecting the cub to be curled up asleep in a corner. But out walked unsteadily a very young tiger cub only a few days old, which I immediately named Rocky.

'Naturally the sudden appearance of a tiny tiger cub created a great deal of excitement, and within a minute I had a dozen customs staff crowding around me asking questions and wanting to take photographs with the small cub. I quickly thanked them for their kind attention, and popped Rocky back into the carrying case and beat a hasty retreat to board the light aircraft.

'Rocky was an Amur tiger who had been rejected by his mother and would have died if we hadn't been able to care for him. When I got Rocky back home, I helped Rachael mix up his feed – the whole day seemed unreal.

'That was the start of a special relationship between myself and Rocky the tiger, and I devoted most of my time to him. I'd be at the park with him during the day and then I'd take him home with me to look after him in the evenings with the help of Rachael. We would stay up till midnight bottle-feeding him every few hours and taking care of his ablutions and all his needs. Then we'd settle him down to get some sleep and set the alarm clock for 4.30 a.m. ready to carry on feeding Rocky and rearing him until he travelled with me back to Paradise.

'It was another huge learning curve for us – how do you keep a cub alive, what sort of milk do they need, what ingredients are required to keep them healthy such as calcium for their bones? Rocky arrived at Paradise weighing 2 lbs (1 kg) and grew to weigh in excess of 35 stone (222 kg).'

Of necessity Peter learned fast, but he also registered himself at Oxford Brookes University to take a course on the management of animals in captivity. One lesson he quickly learned at home was that a growing tiger cub would soon start biting the furniture and chewing playfully at everything in reach. 'It's amazing how quickly they grow. Within a month I was setting Rocky up in a little pen and I was able to slip a lead on him and take him for walks.'

Colin Elcombe, who had started working at Paradise as a young teenager and worked his way up to become head cat keeper, watched in awe as an extraordinary bond developed between Peter and Rocky the tiger cub. He says: 'It was a special time for me working at Paradise where I was a cat keeper. I loved my job, and as Rocky had come from a circus background, in my eyes he was a rescued cat and I knew we would give him a far better life than he would have had anywhere else.

'I worked with Rocky from a young age after Peter had hand-raised him, and in truth I have never met a gentler soul than Rocky. He was so placid and loving, and I would like to think that some of that had rubbed off on him from Peter and myself. I would walk Rocky around the park in the mornings and up into the woods and then Peter and I would sit with him at Tiger Lodge and he would suck Peter's fingers or thumb like a baby as if it was his milk bottle. Rachael wasn't overly impressed with this. She said it made him look silly – she meant Rocky, not Peter! But she knew how happy Rocky was doing just that.

'I hope those mornings sitting with Rocky in the Tiger House were as special for Peter as they were for me,' Colin continues. 'It gave Peter the chance to lay down his welding equipment for once and just be with the animals he loves. During those mornings we would talk and dream about one day having a sanctuary, as all the cats in our care were growing up and we worried about where they would go. We also dreamed of a sanctuary whereby we could play a part in the international breeding programme.'

Such was Peter's involvement in building Paradise Wildlife Park that it took Colin Elcombe some considerable time before he realised that the man busying himself around the park in shorts and khaki shirt, happily getting his hands dirty with all manner of tasks, was in fact the owner of Paradise. 'For a while I thought Peter was just another member of the staff,' Colin says. 'He was constantly running everywhere, welding, concreting, putting up fences, driving the minibus to the station to collect visitors and busying himself in the workshop.

'This man was always diligent, working with his hands and doing everyday jobs and he had a zest for life and clearly loved being alive doing what he was doing. I could tell he wanted to be out working hard on the ground laying the foundations for what Paradise became.'

In his own way, Rocky became a major star of Paradise Wildlife Park when Peter, ever willing to try imaginative new ways of raising money for conservation, dreamed up the daring idea of escorting visitors and guests into a big cat enclosure for a photo opportunity. In conjunction with East Hertfordshire Council, he was able to draw up a special licence giving Paradise permission for just such an up-close encounter inside the enclosure of a young cat, be it a lion, tiger, cheetah or puma.

Foremost among these was Rocky because of his gentle, docile nature, and visitors and guests were happy to pay a contribution to conservation by sitting on a bale of straw and having their photograph taken with Rocky alongside Peter and Colin or on occasions Martin Hill, cat keeper Danny Walker or long-term volunteer Nick Louden. Guests came from all over the world to see the young tigers and lions and to have their photos taken. Memorably, among these visitors was an eighty-five-year-old woman from the Sussex coast. She sat with Peter and Rocky with her hand resting on the tiger and was so moved by the experience that she burst into floods of tears. She explained that she had achieved her lifetime's ambition. It had been her dream since childhood to sit down beside a tiger.

Peter believes that Paradise was the only zoo in the country at the time which held such a licence, and the opportunity of having such a memorable experience proved extraordinarily popular with the visitors. As the word got around, visitors arrived from far and wide specifically to enjoy their unique encounter. Among the visitors who snapped up the chance were many from various countries in Europe, and especially from America.

The one-off licence at Paradise naturally required stringent measures to be put in place for the safety of both the members of the Paradise cat team and the guests venturing into the enclosures. It was agreed in the rules Peter drew up that each guest would always be accompanied by two experienced Paradise cat team members inside the cat's enclosure while a third stood attentively just outside the enclosure with a two-way radio.

Each morning before the pre-booked photo sessions there would be a check on the young tigers and lions to make certain they were content and healthy, ready for the encounters scheduled for the day ahead. 'I always wanted the cats to enjoy the procedure as much as the visitor,' Peter says, 'and there were certain days when a tiger or lion didn't want to participate and I always recognised and respected that. I wouldn't have allowed it if there had been any risk of danger. I could always feel when Rocky, or one of our other cats, for some reason didn't like a particular person. I could feel them tugging on the lead. But generally, the cats got to know the procedure and they enjoyed it.'

Everything went smoothly for two years without incident or alarm until the process came to an abrupt end after Peter had invited the council into Paradise with a view to renewing his unique licence for a further two years. 'On the day the inspection team came round, I was warned that, although they could not stop me from staging my big cat encounters, my zoo licence would be taken away at the first sign of any sort of accident or any hint of a safety scare. The risk for me was too big: we had never had any trouble and I was confident we would have none, but I couldn't afford the risk of losing our zoo licence.'

Peter believes the inspector's decision was swayed by the recent deaths of two cat keepers who had been killed at another animal park in the UK. 'In each case it was down to misadventure in their housekeeping and nothing to do with experiences,' Peter pointed out. 'But our local authority still decided they must put an end to our particular cat experiences. I endeavoured to explain that we had never had an accident, we had a hundred per cent safety record, and the strict safety precautions were always in place. But they were adamant and we were forced to scrap our cat experiences that very same day. I never took anyone into a tiger enclosure ever again.

'With hindsight, I wish we had fought our case or asked for a winding-down period. I felt the local authority and licensing people didn't allow us time to acclimatise Rocky and our other cats to the fact that guests would no longer be spending time with them in their enclosures. It would have been helpful to have had time to wean the cats off these experiences as I felt to end them so abruptly generated a welfare issue for our young lions and tigers. The reality was that the encounters were as much a part of the lives of the cats as they were a part of ours. The cats enjoyed them as much as we did.'

Ultimately the scrapping of the close encounter photo sessions was a bitter blow to fundraising for conservation. 'The popularity of the big cat encounter was such that we were carrying out as many as ten a day,' Peter says. 'Over the two years these experiences raised £100,000. We vowed from the start that all the money from these photo sessions should go towards conservation. We were desperate not to use the money for profit, and we stuck to our guns. Rocky was the star of it all, and every penny of that money raised by him and the other cats went towards conservation of their cousins out in the wild. Rocky's achievements were far greater than ours. Those photo sessions with him probably saved hundreds of tigers in the wild.'

The cancellation of the photo opportunities spurred Peter and the Paradise team on to setting up new experiences for visitors and guests. One such initiative was 'Walking with Wolves', a walk through the woodland pathways in a specially enlarged wolf enclosure house which helped to raise money towards wolf conservation.

Rocky went on to light up Peter's life, and in many ways the lives of Colin Elcombe and the entire team. Rocky spent his entire life at either Paradise or The Big Cat Sanctuary, and he reached the grand old age of nearly twenty by the time he died at Paradise in 2018. All the keepers loved him, but, having nurtured him from when he was a tiny cub just one week old, Peter's bond with Rocky was especially strong.

He says: 'In the days of Rocky's youth, I would either be with him or see him every day and he would respond to my voice. His attitude and disposition was totally different from other tigers. He had his own special nature. He never showed any aggression and he was almost too friendly even when he was fully grown. Even towards the end of his life when age and time had started to take their toll, we still had a great rapport and he still recognised my voice. He could tell when I was coming to see him and I could always stroke him without fear.'

But there came a point when it was all too apparent to Peter, Lynn, head of cats Ian Jones, deputy head of cats Cassie Jones, as well as Shirley Luck and other members of the keeper team that Rocky's health was failing. He became ill for some weeks, becoming weaker, frailer and finding normal life increasingly difficult, slowly going downhill, and his legs were noticeably weakening.

This put Peter in an unenviable quandary. The vet and the keepers could all see Rocky's strength was fading fast, but it was difficult for Peter to convince himself that the tiger's quality of life was so rapidly diminishing that the kindest thing would be to have him put down. That was not how Peter saw the situation and with good reason. Every time he paid Rocky a visit himself, the tiger would recognise his voice and perk up and become lively. To Peter, his beloved tiger seemed mostly to be his normal self, especially on Saturdays when as a treat Martin Hill, who had been a volunteer in the cat section at Paradise, came in with a large salmon for Rocky to tuck into.

Peter was advised, however, that Rocky was a very different tiger when he was not around. Rocky rallied only because there was such a powerful bond between them. 'They told me that when I wasn't there with Rocky he just lay down on the ground all day long and never got up. They believed the right decision was to have him put down, and I felt as if I was almost being encouraged to do that. And yet, whenever I was with him he seemed to be as right as rain.

'With my very different view of Rocky, the implication was that I was wanting to keep him alive for my own sake. But that wasn't the case. When any animal is sickening I try not to make the ultimate decision. But the buck stops with me and if the vet, my family and the team tell me an animal must be put down, I have to accept responsibility. And that was the case with Rocky as by now he could not even stand.'

There were protracted meetings involving the Paradise vet, John Lewis, the entire Paradise cat team and members of the Sampson family. It was a heartbreaking moment for Peter when John urged him the right decision was to have the much-loved tiger put to sleep. Peter acknowledged it was the correct call but naturally it didn't stop him from becoming deeply upset.

'I had to take this terrible decision, and as Rocky's final day dawned I was half praying that John would phone me up and tell me that for some reason he couldn't make it that day to put him down. On that awful day all the Paradise team and Rocky's keepers both past and present were there and I went into his enclosure with John to say my goodbye to Rocky.

'I had tears in my eyes when John first sedated him with an injection before giving him one final lethal dose. As I walked out of the enclosure afterwards I remember I had an awful feeling of guilt that I had killed Rocky, that I was the one who had ended his life. I asked myself: "Why have I done that?" Had I let everyone talk me into having my fantastic tiger, my special friend, put down? I'd have preferred it if Rocky had died from a heart attack in the night. It was such a sad day, without a doubt my saddest time in all the years at Paradise. What added to the deep sorrow for Rachael and me was that on the same day our domestic cat, Purdy, sadly also had to be put down. She was twenty-one years old.

'I hate it when any animal dies. It always upsets me. I know it's inevitable, I know it's going to happen, but it was extremely hard to take with Rocky as we had had such a wonderful connection between us. We had rescued Rocky as a tiny cub at one week old after he had been rejected by his mother. He was small enough then as to fit almost in my pocket. We had bottle-fed him, we had hand-raised him and when he was two years old and fully grown, he was still sucking my thumb like a baby.

'For nearly twenty years we had cared for him and given him a happy life. At zoo conventions the general opinion is that tigers live for around ten years in the wild where, of course, there are always dangers to life – they do not have veterinary care, they are hunted, poisoned, shot by poachers and have genetic problems through mixed breeding. So by rescuing Rocky he was able to enjoy twice the life span he would have had in the wild.

'I would put the longevity of his life down to the love, affection and care he was shown by all our team at Paradise and The Big Cat Sanctuary. Rocky had a great life, he was the flagship species of Paradise, and he brought us lots of enjoyment. I love all the animals but I was especially close to Rocky and because of the grief I felt with his death I try desperately not to get too close to animals anymore.'

Rocky was a great ambassador for Paradise Wildlife Park, for The Big Cat Sanctuary and for conservation following in the paw prints of Bobby the lion several years earlier. Peter still keeps Rocky's ashes on his sideboard and has a little statue of him as a permanent reminder. Legendary sculptor Steve Winterburn, who created the stunning sculpture of five football legends at Wembley stadium, marked Peter's extraordinary close relationship with his beloved Rocky by crafting a magnificent bronze sculpture of them together which stands on display at Hertfordshire Zoo.

* * *

One day Peter was contacted by a man who lived near Exmoor in Devon, who explained he was going through a divorce and needed to rehome some of his animal stock. Would Peter be interested in a pair of pumas? The answer was yes, and Peter hired a large van and accompanied by Alan Wright, a maintenance worker at the park, he drove down to Devon, where he was introduced to the pumas. 'While the owner went off to his house to bring me the paperwork, I opened the gate to the pumas' enclosure and let myself in,' Peter recalls. 'I had assumed that the pumas were used to someone regularly going into their enclosure but they did not seem overly happy to see me and when they started to take too close an interest in me all I had to protect myself with was a broom I was able to grab. The next thing I knew, the owner came running down the garden shouting in alarm for me to get out of the enclosure. He had never once been inside with them, and nor had anyone else.

'With difficulty we managed to load the two pumas into large carrying crates and the owner also gave us a little puma cub, which he brought out in a large shoebox. We had the cub with us in the cab on the way back to Paradise. Once we had settled the pumas in at our park, I was able to go into their enclosure with them each day and they were perfectly happy with my presence.

'We were going to run a naming competition for the puma cub with the help of two people who had become good friends – Paul 'Gazza' Gascoigne, the Spurs and England football superstar, and model Linda Lusardi, but the cub turned out to be a young male, so he was named Gazza. If it had been a female she should have been called Linda.'

***

It says much about Peter's standing in the zoo world that by the 1990s he was welcomed as a member of the British and Irish Association of Zoos and Aquariums (BIAZA). This is an organisation dedicated to achieving the highest standards of animal care, to conserving the natural world through research and conservation, and to educating and inspiring their visitors. Membership of the European Association of Zoos and Aquariums (EAZA) followed in 1991 and eventually a prestigious membership of the World Association of Zoos and Aquariums (WAZA), an honour earned by few British zoos.

In time Peter was elected to sit on the main BIAZA council and one of his roles was to be part of the Membership and Licensing Committee for new members. This involved him inspecting other zoos which had applied to be members as well as visiting existing members to check on standards and animal welfare. In time Steve, Lynn and grandson Tyler became members of the BIAZA Council too.

As Peter started to become more involved within the zoo world in general, he travelled regularly throughout Europe with Rachael, visiting zoos in the Netherlands, Belgium, France, Germany, the Czech Republic and Poland. On each trip he was making friends and contacts with people and organisations who shared his commitment to conservation. On a visit to Sweden he journeyed on to Helsinki to meet and subsequently forge a great friendship with Leif Blanqvist, the studbook keeper for snow leopards, which led eventually to snow leopards arriving at both Paradise Wildlife Park and The Big Cat Sanctuary.

Thanks to the sale of his coach and travel business and other assets, Peter had the funds necessary to create an animal park to the standard he wanted, with education and conservation at its core. All through the 1990s, together with the full support of his family, he ploughed his energy into upgrading and landscaping the animal paddocks and enclosures, putting up new fencing and gates, and building four double-ended stable blocks to house camels, zebras, llamas, tapirs and wolves – and much else besides.

Helping to fund wildlife artists in Africa and backing Project Life Lion were just two of a large number of major conservation initiatives Peter threw his support behind. Project Life Lion was launched in 1995 following the emergence of the shattering statistic that around 2,000 lions and other animals had died from canine distemper. As a consequence, Paradise played a major role, spearheaded by Steve Sampson, in helping to support and fund the mass vaccination against rabies and other diseases of semi-wild dogs owned by the local population living on the borders of the Serengeti National Pak in Tanzania and Kenya.

While Peter endeavoured to strike a balance between improving and upgrading the park and bringing in more animals and supporting and funding a wide range of conservation initiatives, work continued of necessity on Paradise's infrastructure. The main driveway and car parks had to be levelled and tarmacked, which was carried out by close friend Steve Candler, or as known to Peter, Steve Tarmac. It enabled the park to take on a much more professional look. In addition, the electricity needed upgrading more than once at great expense and a sizeable generator was installed as backup.

A large toilet block was built to the side of the main car park, large enough to include two disabled toilets and baby-changing facilities. As public attendance at the park accelerated another toilet block was sited on the animal park itself. This required the installation of a new sewerage system with an extra-large septic tank. In conjunction with the tank's manufacturers, Peter had to work out beforehand the number of visitors the park was likely to attract, the number of staff on-site, and how he envisaged the park would grow, before deciding on the size of the hole that needed to be dug to house the sewerage unit. 'You could have parked a double-decker bus in it,' he says, 'and that was only the start as trenches had to be dug to connect up the new system, with builder Ray Chapman as the driving force.

Over time Paradise had its own water supply, its own sewerage system, upgraded electricity and large Calor Gas tanks around the site to make up for the lack of mains gas.

'It always seemed strange to me,' Peter says on reflection, 'that our Paradise Wildlife Park location was right in the middle of Broxbourne woods and yet when you stood at our main gates and looked south, you could see the tower blocks of north London.'

While a sound infrastructure was essential, Peter was conscious at the same time to make improvements at Paradise for the benefit of families visiting with young children. His ingenuity and vision, coupled with opportunism and a can-do approach to the most difficult of transport challenges, saw the purchase of two fire engines, which became suitably themed, a gypsy caravan, and a disused ferry boat which had taken people across the Thames on the outskirts of London. When converted, the old ferry became Pirate's Cove, a popular attraction topped only by a 30-tonne old shunting engine purchased from the London docks which became Thomas the Tank Engine.

The creation of a large timber adventure playground followed, then a special playground for children with disabilities, and a woodland railway complete with station. In addition, a large hay and straw barn was converted into a tiered seated theatre with animal shows, mainly for children.

***

There were many highlights for Peter in the 1990s, not just with the animals. In the space of under four years he was thrilled to become a grandfather four times over. His first grandson, Aaron, was born to daughter Lynn and Craig on 13 November 1991. He was followed by a second grandson, Tyler, on 15 April 1993, and a third boy, Cameron, on 15 July 1995. In between, on 7 August 1994, son Steve's wife Angela gave birth to Scott. All four grandsons went on to contribute to the success of Paradise. 'Happy days,' says Peter. 'In a relatively short time I had four wonderful grandsons. But there was sadness too when shortly after Tyler was born my mother died in May 1995. That was an extremely sad day and a great loss to me and my family. Looking back into the past, for many years it had just been my mother and me together and I always wonder if I could have done more for her.'

It came as a surprise to Peter just prior to the new millennium when Lynn and Craig looked into moving with their three sons to Australia. Craig was from Sydney and Canberra, and had relatives there, so they would have a base from which to build a new life. To help towards their moving expenses, Peter agreed to buy Pembridge Banqueting Ltd, the catering business that Lynn had built up on-site. Over time this had proved to be very successful for Sunday lunches, weddings, the nightclub and various events as well as the day-to-day cafeteria. Steve's wife Angela stepped into managing the catering side of Paradise in Lynn's place. But on reconsideration Lynn and Craig made the decision not to move to Australia and Lynn happily resumed work alongside her father, running Paradise Wildlife Park and The Big Cat Sanctuary.

CHAPTER TEN
Claws Out at Marley Farm

'You're not going to buy Marley Farm – I am'
– *Peter Sampson to the Born Free Foundation*

Ask those closest to Peter Sampson what they believe he would most like to be remembered for, and each and every one without hesitation will offer the same reply: 'The Big Cat Sanctuary.'

'That's his soul, that's his legacy,' says Peter's partner Rachael. 'The Big Cat Sanctuary is not just an offshoot of Paradise Wildlife Park, now Hertfordshire Zoo. This is Peter. This is what he's all about.'

For those unfamiliar with The Big Cat Sanctuary (BCS), it can be described in its simplest form as a UK-based conservation charity dedicated to the preservation, breeding and care of exotic wild cats. Situated in 32 acres deep in the Kent countryside, it is currently home to over fifty big and small cats across sixteen different species, many of which are classed as more than vulnerable to the risk of extinction on the Red List of the International Union for Conservation (IUCN). The cats at BCS comprise the most diverse collection in the UK.

It is a centre of excellence whose primary objective is the breeding of some of the most endangered species on the planet as well as offering sanctuary to retired and rescue cats.

'Protection is our passion' is the proud slogan of BCS, and there is no doubt it is Peter's life force which has been and still is driving the BCS breeding programme along with his family and its campaign to raise awareness and funding for big cat and other wildlife conservation projects around the world.

'It's the conservation and protection of something that is so fragile that appeals to Peter,' explains Rachael. 'That's what he's struggled to achieve against great adversity at The Big Cat Sanctuary, including initially from the local council. But he hung on in there and won them over and he won't stop till he achieves his goals.

'These cats are in such limited numbers in the world right now, and in the future they could be non-existent. That's why Peter's work is so important. He realises that these beautiful animals that he's so in tune with are going to be gone unless we all do something to prevent it. It's their vulnerability that is a challenge to Peter. Animals will accept kindness and that element appeals to Peter and gives him great joy.

'There is something in his character that connects with nature, and it's a side of him that I don't think he was fully aware of in the beginning. It's the fragility of big cats and their conservation which is a challenge to him.'

Peter has no doubts about his calling: 'Like many people, I find it so sad watching TV programmes showing the habitats of these big cats fast disappearing, and they're still being shot, poisoned, trapped, destroyed. I look at these beautiful animals and think that in maybe twenty years' time there won't be any left in the wild. And when it comes to raising money for their conservation, there are times when I wonder whether I'm trying to push a boulder uphill with my nose. All I know is, I've got to keep trying.'

The extraordinary backstory of Peter's creation of BCS at Marley Farm, in Smarden, Kent, dates back to 1990, fully eleven years before its inauguration under its previous name of the Wildlife Heritage Foundation. And it all began when beleaguered Maidstone Borough Council were forced to put out a desperate plea for someone to look after two lions.

It's fair to say that the busy council offices in Maidstone, Kent, were never built with the idea in mind that one day they might have to serve as temporary lodgings for two mighty kings of the jungle. But that was the stark reality facing Maidstone council officials in the summer of 1990 when right out of the blue they were called out to a travelling circus appearing at the Kent county showground in the small village of Detling. They had been alerted to safety fears about the two lions which were the star attractions of the circus.

The two big cats were in what the council called a 'beast wagon' which on inspection was deemed to be unsafe, and council administrators felt they had no option but to take possession of the animals rather than risk any sort of danger to the public.

But what were they to do with them? Suddenly having two lions in their possession was the unlikeliest of headaches for the council, and in desperation they were forced to issue a public appeal for anyone suitably qualified to take them off their hands and care for them.

At first the lions were transported to Longleat Safari Park in Wiltshire for safe and proper care, but it was only a temporary haven. Longleat soon decided they were unable to keep them on a permanent basis and with nowhere else to go their fate seemed sealed.

It was at this point that a part-time farmer in Kent by the name of Malcolm Dudding learned of their predicament and generously volunteered to give both lions a home. Luckily for these two big cats, Malcolm owned a 42-acre site of prime countryside deep in the heart of Kent at Smarden, near Ashford, where he kept rare African cattle and American bison. Even more fortunately for the lions, these cattle breeds were classified as dangerous wild animals and, in order to keep them, Malcolm had obtained a licence under the Dangerous Wild Animal Act (DWA). In possession of a bona fide DWA licence Malcolm was therefore in a position to ask Ashford Borough Council for permission to broaden the terms of the licence to enable him to keep wild cats on the premises in addition to his other animals.

Consent was granted by a grateful Maidstone council, and Malcolm further extended his act of mercy to the two lions by building a special enclosure for them at a cost of several thousand pounds. It was an exceptionally generous undertaking since Malcolm had originally set aside that considerable sum for the addition of a utility room to be built on to the side of his bungalow. This particular domestic building project was subsequently abandoned, and the lion enclosure turned out to be the first of many to be built on the site in years to come.

While Malcolm was building the enclosure, the two lions were transferred for a brief period to London Zoo. There they were gratefully received into a new lion terrace which had recently been built at the zoo but with as yet no lions to show for it. London Zoo was awaiting the arrival of several lions so Malcolm's big cats were doubly welcome as temporary attractions. While they were at London Zoo, the lions were given an extensive health check including examination by a veterinary dentist which revealed that both animals were around fifteen years old.

The two big cats subsequently arrived at Marley Farm the following year, in 1991, together with a third, a lioness Malcolm had taken pity on and rescued after he had travelled to Longleat to collect his original two. He learned from Longleat's manager that there was a lioness which wouldn't go into the pride at the park and she had therefore been moved in with Malcolm's pair. On enquiring what would happen to the lioness if he took just his two lions away, Malcolm was informed that she would have to be put down as she could not be kept on her own. Malcolm immediately agreed to take this lioness to Marley Farm as well.

Malcolm's collection soon grew to five when he gave a home to two more lions from Windsor Safari Park when it closed down in 1994. He had another enclosure built with the help of two charities and various animal welfare groups, including the Born Free Foundation.

A further two lions arrived in 1995 thanks to the BBC reality programme *Challenge Anneka*, hosted by the popular presenter Anneka Rice. The format of the show involved Anneka persuading companies and individuals to contribute their time and resources for free to accomplish a set task within a strict time limit. The task was normally carried out in aid of a charitable or worthy cause, and in this instance Anneka found herself challenged by the Born Free Foundation to rescue two neglected lions from a zoo in Athens and have them transported to a newly built enclosure at Marley Farm – all within a timescale of just sixty-one hours.

Millions of viewers watched enthralled as Anneka went off to Greece to collect the two lions, Gilda and Ivan, from their cramped conditions in what was effectively just an aviary. Meanwhile, all the participating contractors contributing to the TV programme worked hard for three days to transform a field at Marley Farm into a purpose-built enclosure fit for lions.

Anneka's accomplishment of the task was a resounding success in every way. She completed the challenge within the time limit, the programme attracted a huge TV audience, and Gilda and Ivan were able to start a new life in rural Kent under the joint protection of Malcolm Dudding and Born Free.

Approximately two years after the programme was transmitted, Peter's son Steve paid Marley Farm a visit to observe the workings of Malcolm Dudding's big cat operation and he soon realised that Malcolm could do with some financial assistance. The sanctuary was not being run as a commercial operation and it was extremely expensive to manage. 'So, I decided with Dad to help Malcolm out,' Steve says. 'I left him my calling card, and we sent him a cheque to help buy meat to feed the cats and thought no more about it.'

Nearly two years later, when Malcolm was having problems with Born Free, he found Steve's card, which he had tucked behind a clock on the mantlepiece, and telephoned him to ask if the Sampsons would be interested in buying Marley Farm. 'The call came right out of the blue,' says Steve. 'One of the very best things I've ever been able to do for my dad was to walk into his office and say: "How do you fancy becoming Born Free's landlord?"'

The sudden availability of the site to the Sampson family was a direct result of the family's generosity in helping Malcolm financially – and it could not have come at a better time for Peter. He had limited space at Paradise Wildlife Park and was desperate to expand with big cat conservation in mind. He had considered taking on a second zoo but it would have been nigh on impossible to run two operations the size of Paradise Wildlife Park at the same time. Zoos are cash businesses and require hands-on management.

Peter and Steve had in fact gone as far as to take a look at several other sites, small zoos and other animal collections, but none had fitted in with their plans. 'We spent eighteen months looking for an additional site for the cats in our care,' Peter says. 'We weren't looking to open another zoo like Paradise, but more of a sanctuary. Although we found one or two locations that we thought were ideal, sadly they were far more expensive than our funds would allow.'

The Smarden site, now with several lions already in residence, stimulated Peter's interest, because his love of big cats had grown into a passion for them ever since his instinctive mercy dash to ease Bobby the lion's suffering as soon as he had acquired Broxbourne Zoo.

At Malcolm's invitation, Peter paid his first visit to Marley Farm as a potential buyer, and initially he had his doubts. 'The site back then was essentially a muddy field flanked by a railway line on one side and an industrial estate beyond a small wood on the other side, and there was an airfield nearby. I was just getting Paradise Wildlife Park up and running and I thought to myself that I already owned a site at Broxbourne which I needed to develop so did I really want another one? A further consideration was that Kent seemed to me to be so far away, on the other side of the country from Broxbourne.

'Malcolm related to me the story of how he had rescued the original two lions and how Ashford Council had given him permission to build enclosures and had granted him a DWA licence for them. He also explained that over several years he had allowed Born Free to share the site with him but he felt that relations between them had lately cooled somewhat and that they were trying to get him out.

'He felt Born Free were trying to take over,' says Peter, 'and revealed they had made him an offer to purchase the site. I spent the day having a good look round and speaking to one or two people and, to be honest, I wasn't overly impressed with what I saw. Horses were being slaughtered to utilise the meat for the cats but the smell was terrible and so were the conditions in my opinion.'

Peter asked Malcolm for a few days in which to consider his options and arranged to make a return visit to Marley Farm one week later. At the end of that week he was still undecided. 'Bearing in mind that we had so much work to do at Paradise Wildlife Park, I wondered if this investment would be a step too far. I was also genuinely concerned about the travelling and the journeys I would have to make to get from Hertfordshire to the depths of Kent. The radius was important because we didn't want to be a hundred miles from Paradise.' But Marley Farm was approximately 70 miles from Paradise.

Despite his misgivings, Peter could see the Smarden site offered real potential, the main advantage being that it already had several enclosures. That suited Peter's plans to reorganise the cat collection at Paradise Wildlife Park by reducing the number of tigers and introducing new animals such as jaguars and leopards.

'On the day of my return visit,' he recalls, 'I came across a couple of representatives from Born Free who must have got wind that Malcolm had spoken to me about the possibility of my buying Marley Farm. In conversation with them they were adamant: "There is no way you'll be able to buy the site," were their exact words, "because we're buying it."'

That was like a red rag to a bull for Peter. His competitive instincts kicked into overdrive. 'I was on the point of carrying on with just Paradise Wildlife Park, but when I was informed that Born Free were trying to buy Marley Farm, I thought "No you're not, because I'm going to buy it!" Even then, I still had my doubts.'

Peter immediately sought out Malcolm and told him he was happy to buy Marley Farm at the price he was suggesting. 'I also assured Malcolm that there would always be a place for him at Marley Farm – and there still is. He lives in the bungalow with his family and Dely, his wife, still works with us at The Big Cat Sanctuary, on the edge of the farm. We shook hands, and other than having the deal formalised by solicitors, I thought it was done.' But far from it.

Peter's purchase of Marley Farm proved to be a long, drawn out, highly complicated and contested process which stretched over the best part of two years. 'It was like pulling teeth,' he says. 'I almost gave up so many times.' It transpired that Marley Farm was in fact owned by a family trust and it took a long time for solicitors to unpick it all and for everyone to agree.

There followed a legal tussle between Peter and the Born Free Foundation which centred on what legitimate rights, if any, Born Free claimed on the property following the *Challenge Anneka* rescue. 'Born Free claimed they had a lease on the land,' Peter explains, 'but when I asked them to show me the paperwork for the lease it became apparent there was none. They had just a verbal agreement with Malcolm Dudding to simply use enclosures on the site for their cats.

'Born Free argued their case and insisted that legally they had a right to stay. But after more meetings with Malcolm and our solicitors, it was established that nothing had ever been put in writing, nothing had ever been formally agreed. It was more down to Malcolm's kindness rather than a formal arrangement with Born Free that had allowed them to share Marley Farm with him.

'When I met Born Free again and explained the situation to them, they said they had solicitors and barristers who were friends of Born Free who would work for them to sort out the issue and that the matter could take several years to be settled through the courts.'

Negotiations to resolve issues proved exceptionally complex – and potentially extremely costly for Peter. It left him facing huge legal bills the longer everything remained uncertain and contested. 'Born Free had top lawyers on the case, but I had just a local solicitor,' he points out, 'and when I asked him how long the consultations might go on for and what the legal fees might amount to, he said it could take several years and cost me a substantial amount, many thousands of pounds. I said I'd rather spend that amount of money on the cats. Our solicitor urged me to reach an amicable agreement.'

As negotiations dragged on, Peter lost count of the times people told him he was wasting his time with regards to Born Free. But that made him all the more determined to reach an agreement with them. He stayed strong in his pursuit of the site because he had the vision that the land could provide somewhere suitable for his conservation and breeding aspirations. Moreover, he had the confidence and self-belief that he was fully capable of fulfilling his dreams.

There followed two years of difficult negotiations with Born Free. Eventually Peter offered Born Free a compromise. 'As I had now purchased the site, I offered them the opportunity that I would look after their two lions for free and cover their veterinary cost and feed. The Born Free hierarchy were quite keen on this idea,' Peter recalls, 'but their members didn't like it.'

True to the ethos of their organisation, Born Free Foundation's members were understandably uneasy about sharing the premises with the owners of a zoo. 'At Paradise Wildlife Park we were a zoo and the antithesis of what Born Free is all about,' says Peter. 'They want zoos to shut down, they feel animals should be living in the wild — which I don't totally disagree with and wish it could be so today.

'A further stumbling block to this deal was that Born Free were not prepared for us to do any breeding of big cats. "But that's what we do!" I protested. I attended several meetings with Born Free at their headquarters and fully explained that Marley Farm was not going to be a zoo as such but a conservation centre for some of the cats we had at Paradise. It would also be a rescue centre and a breeding centre for endangered big cats.'

For Peter to follow through with his ambitions he would require a DWA licence at Marley Farm, and in an effort to solve the impasse he suggested a meeting with Ashford Council to explain the situation fully. 'That meeting did not go well,' Peter recalls. 'The council seemed to be totally in favour of Born Free and not happy with myself or Paradise Wildlife Park. They loved Born Free, who were represented at the meeting, but they looked daggers at us. They thought Born Free were nice people, but they didn't like me. It was a case of "Who the hell are you?" I had to explain what we do, and what we are about.

'After further negotiations it was agreed that we could have a twelve-month DWA licence in joint names. So we had Paradise Wildlife Park and the Born Free Foundation registered together on the licence — which must have struck a nerve with Born Free as part of their ethos was to have zoos closed down. However, the council agreed to grant my half of the licence only so long as it was reviewed every year. They also imposed numerous conditions and the licensing officer, Sheila Davidson, said she would monitor the progress over the coming twelve months.

'During that period we registered the name of the Wildlife Heritage Foundation and at numerous council meetings over that year I stressed we had no interest in opening up a wildlife park similar to Paradise. We just wanted a conservation and breeding centre for cats which would not be open to the general public.

'After that first twelve months of operating with a joint DWA licence, we met again with Ashford Council for our review and Sheila Davidson was so much more positive with us. She said we had achieved more in one year than Born Free had in several. She said we had made very good progress in putting the place in a far better shape. It was then agreed that we would become the sole operator on the DWA licence as we were the ones who had carried out all the work to meet the conditions that had not been previously completed. Thus there was no need to have Born Free on the licence, plus we were the owners. We had in fact made an exceptionally good start at Marley Farm and in meeting with Born Free I explained the position and said if they wished still to have two enclosures and home the rescued cats then I and my team would look after them.'

After much debate, Born Free decided they wanted to leave Marley Farm but as they felt they had invested in it, they asked for a very high settlement fee to move on. 'That was about four and a half times the amount we had in mind,' Peter says. 'We finally settled on a figure which was still a great deal of money for me at the time. It was still an extremely difficult time for us financially, as we were trying to upgrade and develop Paradise as well as get Marley Farm off the ground. When we shook hands with Born Free and agreed on the deal, I had to tell them that I didn't have the money, as the settlement was pretty expensive for me. We agreed to a payment plan of so much a year, over seven years. We took this on board, and we were true to our word and completed it in the time frame.'

The formalities were officially finalised at a meeting in London with all parties concerned. Generously, after a long, frustrating and fractious period, Peter gave Born Free no deadline for ending their practical association with Marley Farm. 'There's no rush,' I said, 'you have a couple of cats homed at the farm and I will care for them.'

Happily, after such protracted, fraught negotiations, Peter has no ill feelings whatsoever towards Born Free. 'In fairness, I have a lot of respect for what Born Free does and stands for. But I have a lot of respect for what we do too,' he stresses. 'To be fair, Born Free found it difficult as they were only interested in rescues not in creating a centre for conservation and breeding like we were.'

Once Peter had ownership and full control of the site, he predictably still faced strong opposition from the local parish council when he outlined his ambitious plans for the expansion of Marley Farm into the Wildlife Heritage Foundation (WHF), later renamed Big Cat Sanctuary (BCS) in 2018, a registered conservation charity dedicated to the preservation, breeding and care of exotic big cats. He stated it would be a sanctuary for, among others, Amur leopards, Bengal tigers, Amur tigers, cheetahs, African lions, snow leopards, Sumatran tigers and Pallas's cats.

Peter made his plans and goals for the site perfectly clear. 'As we needed to build new facilities, I set up a meeting with Martin Vink, who was head of planning at Ashford Council at the time. I found him to be hard but fair and he allowed me to explain fully our long-term aims with the WHF. I wanted it to be a sanctuary for cats, large and small, and I stressed that we did not intend for it to be open to the general public.'

With the help of expensively drawn up plans and designs, Peter submitted a planning application which would include building larger houses and enclosures for not just the cats currently in their care but for more cats to arrive in the future. With one or two alterations Martin Vink was prepared to put Peter's plans forward for approval by the planning committee.

But there was deep disappointment when the Smarden Parish Council objected. 'I don't believe they understood what we were endeavouring to create,' Peter stated. 'I remember one of the local objectors saying she didn't want another Alton Towers on her doorstep. Sadly, our application was declined. In fairness to Martin Vink at Ashford Council, he felt our proposals were feasible with the conditions we were imposing upon ourselves and we should consider going for an appeal – which we did.

'It took several weeks for our appeal to be heard, and I was able to show an assessor around and explain to him what we endeavoured to do. He subsequently met with one of the local neighbours who had objected to our plans. I was not allowed to attend but my colleague Alan Philpott and the assessor met with her, and the assessor left informing me I could expect a decision in six to eight weeks. He gave the impression that all was fine, but two weeks later we were informed we had lost the appeal.'

One local resident had expressed grave misgivings at the idea of big cats setting up home in the verdant heartland of the county that prides itself on its reputation as 'the garden of England'. She needed to be persuaded that Peter's plans were environmentally acceptable and that the husbandry of so many big cats would be carried out with safety as paramount. Crucial to the approval of Peter's plans was his insistence that the site would not be open to the general public although there might be occasional open days to show the world what he was doing for conservation.

Again, Peter stressed this would be no theme park with kiddie rides and big dippers. This was strictly to be a project for the conservation and breeding of endangered big cats and a breeding centre of excellence using stock made available and officially approved by the European Endangered Species Programmes (EEP). Peter even offered to write his own rules, terms and conditions for scrutiny so any concerns would be allayed, which he did.

Eventually he won everyone round. Peter's cause was possibly helped by his threat to pull out of Marley Farm if he was barred from building new enclosures and prevented from bringing the site up to professional standards. He followed up this very real threat to abandon his project by casually and judiciously dropping into the discussions that if he simply gave up, there were members of a travelling community who were showing keen interest as potential buyers. The idea of dozens of caravans rolling on to Marley Farm was certainly something for the locals to consider, and they mostly did so with some apprehension.

'I did feel that we had made them think differently,' Peter believes, 'especially when they realised they would not be getting a zoo, as such, in their neighbourhood. I was asked to re-submit our application once more with one or two minor changes and I was thrilled when our plans were approved at the next council meeting.'

Throughout all the planning battles, Peter faced at times fierce opposition from local residents and from various other quarters and he suffered many personal verbal attacks on him and on his integrity which he found particularly hurtful. But he says, 'Since those early days we have had an excellent working relationship with both Smarden Parish Council and Ashford Borough Council as well as with the locals. The councils have both been most helpful, and they are now proud to be associated with us.'

BCS currently issues an annual invitation to all the mayors of Kent to gather at the sanctuary in all their finery for a day hosted by Peter and his team to show them around and what they continue to achieve. The mayors are only too pleased to accept the invitation and count the day out as a highlight of their year. It is proof of their support and admiration for all Peter's and the team's efforts and helps to spread the word about the work of BCS.

***

Peter spent the first few years at Marley Farm welding, repairing and erecting fences, revamping existing enclosures and building new ones. He also cut the grass, constructed pathways and organised the planting of many trees and shrubs to transform the sanctuary with the help of the teams from BCS and Paradise.

Once or twice a week Peter would leave at 6 a.m. to travel from Broxbourne, taking with him a team of at least six members of the staff from Paradise Wildlife Park to carry out new works and improvements, gradually ticking off the list of requirements to meet the conditions of Ashford Council's licensing department.

Weekends saw Peter heading back to the site with Rachael, her father Ray, and her mother Barbara in a large crew cab tipper truck packed with tools and materials. Life became easier for them all at weekends after Peter's application to park a mobile home on the site was granted, which meant they could travel to the site late on Fridays and stay over in some comfort until Sunday.

***

At a later date Peter purchased a motorhome for himself and Rachael and then, with the love of the open road, they began travelling not just within the UK but to various destinations in Europe too. 'When time allowed, we would travel from Land's End to John O'Groats,' Peter says, 'always visiting zoos and wildlife parks, making contacts, getting to know members of staff at each location and meeting up with people who over time became firm friends. There was always something new to be learned at every stop and we were building our knowledge as we went along.'

For their first trip abroad in their new motorhome, Peter and Rachael chose to head over the Channel and make their way down to the south of France. It should have been an unforgettable maiden outing but it is remembered for all the wrong reasons.

Having reached the outskirts of Marseilles it was time for an overnight stop and Peter pulled off road into the large parking area of a motorway service station alongside several other parked motorhomes and caravans. They were ready for a good night's sleep after a long drive. But when they awoke next morning, they were shocked to find they had fallen victim to the nasty tactic of burglars pumping anaesthetic gas into motorhomes to knock their victims out while they helped themselves to anything of any value. The robbers had got away with Peter's and Rachael's watches, some jewellery, mobile phone, travel bags and all the local currency they had taken out for their trip. There was at least a little comfort in that they appeared to have suffered no real physical harm and the thieves had failed to steal their passports, which had been safely stowed away at the back of a cupboard. 'We didn't suffer any after effects from the gassing,' Peter remembers thankfully. 'But it was a horrible fright to wake up to find we'd been robbed like that. We now had no money, and it was such a frightening experience that we thought about just giving up and driving home. But we felt that as we had come that far we would carry on to a campsite near Nice and try and sort things out from there. Which we did.'

When Peter and Rachael reported the crime, the French police did not seem overly interested. It transpired that the injecting of anaesthetic gas into the air conditioning or through windows and under doors of tourists' motorhomes and long-distance lorries was a tactic that was not uncommon at the time among villains operating in the Marseilles region. Tourists were their obvious targets, and Peter and Rachael were just two more unlucky travellers to add to the list of those who suffered this extremely unpleasant experience.

Despite such an alarming incident, undaunted they continued to journey into Europe every year, taking in zoos and animal parks in Switzerland, Belgium, Germany and the Netherlands as well as France. Two locations in

Peter with five-time Speedway World Champion Barry Briggs, whom Peter was proud to be partnered with at Swindon Speedway, and who is now a lifetime friend

Peter with legends of speedway – Broady, Kingy, Colin, Bill, Freddy and Vic

Peter and Bert Harkins promoting the Speedway Museum and the World Speedway Riders' Association

Chris, Peter and Weits, from South Africa, with Nala, our young white lioness, at PWP

Peter with James Musinguzi, Director of UWEC Uganda,
a dear friend, colleague and conservationist, during Peter's visit to Uganda

Ty, Cam and Aaron with the Jeep Animal Ambulance
donated to UWEC Uganda

Peter's seventieth birthday celebrating with the whole gang
(T-B: Peter with Russell and Jo; with Debbie and Alan; with family)

One of our many donations to our conservation partners around the globe (pictured, a donation to the African Wildlife Foundation)

Rachael, Alma and Dame Judi Dench at BCS

Peter with HRH Princess Eugenie, patron of the Big Cat Sanctuary

Peter at the White Lion habitat at BCS with patron Princess Eugenie, Lynn, Sir Eric Peacock, chair of trustees, and Giles Clark, ambassador of BCS

Ambassador and good friend of BCS Paul Hollywood

Peter with trustee and long-time family friend Steve Winterburn, world-renowned sculptor and artist

Having fun! Peter with Sir Eric Peacock and Matt Brady (trustee) – both BCS and PWP (HZ)

Peter, Steve Candler (Steve Tarmac) and good friend Alan Murphy

Peter with Maya, star of *Big Cats About the House* at BCS

Opening of the Amazon and Beyond – Sir Eric Peacock, Sir Charles Walker and Alan Philpott with Lynn and Peter.

THURSDAY, APRIL 14, 2022 MERCURY 13

News

Prime Minister goes back to the age of dinosaurs

By LIBERTY SHELDON
liberty.sheldon@reachplc.com
@liberty_sheldon

ONE of Hertfordshire's most beloved attractions played host to the Prime Minister as he visited the county on Monday morning.

The Prime Minister visited Paradise Wildlife Park with his wife Carrie and his children Wilfred and Romy.

Mr Johnson and his family enjoyed the park's brand-new dinosaurs in the World Of Dinosaurs attraction where they saw more than 40 life-size and moving animatronic dinosaurs.

During their visit, the family were greeted by several onlookers and other visitors who stopped to take photographs with the Prime Minister.

Mr Johnson toured a display of roaring dinosaurs at the park, set to be renamed as Hertfordshire Zoo in 2024 to mark its 40th anniversary.

A spokesperson for Paradise Wildlife Park said: "Boris and his family thoroughly enjoyed taking a trip back through the prehistoric era witnessing more than 40 life size, moving and roaring spectacular animatronic dinosaurs.

"As well as, venturing into the newly-opened area which displays the scariest dinosaur around the Indominus Rex.

"With the chance to jump into the Dino Jeep and have fun escaping the T-Rex this was a family fun filled day the Johnsons could enjoy as they brought the sunshine with them on this Easter week.

"As Boris and the family walked around Paradise Wildlife Park, they were greeted by many excited guests who Boris happily stopped multiple times to have a few photos with.

"The family left Paradise Wildlife Park filled with smiles and excitement from the World of Dinosaurs and the adventures they had."

Mr. Johnson's visit to Paradise Wildlife Park follows his return from a trip to Ukraine, where he toured the country's war-torn capital with President Zelensky.

CEO Lynn Whitnall, Prime Minister Boris Johnson and owner and founder Peter Sampson
PARADISE WILDLIFE PARK

Former prime minister Boris Johnson on a surprise family visit to PWP

Three of Peter's grandsons with *One Zoo Three* on CBBC and BBC iPlayer – the number one children's programme through 2024

Precious first great-grandson Alfie, born to Ty and Carly on 6 December 2023. He is a little gem!

The opening of the IUCN Native Species Trail to commemorate PWP and HZ – the UK's first Centre of Species Survival for Native and Endemic Species, with High Sheriff Annie Brewster

Peter with son Steve and grandson Scott, who is serving in the British Army

Peter with Angela, Steve, Barry and Jan Bright

Peter with Rachael, Laura and granddaughter Lily

Rachael with Andrew and grandson Jayden,
granddaughters Summer and Lily, and Bella the dog

Celebrating forty wild years – 'Keep happy, keep smiling!' – with family and friends

Peter with Tyler, Lewis Cocking (MP for Broxbourne), Mark Mills-Bishop (Hertfordshire County Council), Rachael and Lynn. Lewis is opening the new gibbon habitat at HZ, Song of the Forest

Unveiling of Peter with Rocky the tiger statue to commemorate forty years of Paradise and HZ and all the amazing work

Yuna arrived with shell shock, struggling to walk – she is now a lion reborn (BCiC)

Rori walking on grass for the first time – Big Cats in Crisis Campaign

Cam, Peter, General Valerii Zaluzhnyi of the Ukrainian Army, Ambassador of Ukraine to the UK, Paul Hollywood, Baroness Hayman, Under-Secretary of State at DEFRA, and Lynn

Craig, Tyler, Carly, little Alfie, Rachael, Peter, Cam, Grace, Aaron and Lynn

France's Loire valley, Zoo Parc Beauval and Zoo Doue La Fontaine, became particular favourites where they formed lasting friendships. The latter held particular fascination as it was built into rock on the side of an old quarry and thus prided itself as the only troglodyte zoo in the world.

* * *

In sheer practical terms, juggling efforts to rebuild the old Broxbourne Zoo into Paradise Wildlife Park at the same time as trying to convert Marley Farm into what eventually became the Wildlife Heritage Foundation was never going to be easy for Peter. Without help he would be unable to keep a firm hand and tight control over both at the same time. 'To say it was extremely difficult financially is an understatement,' he says. 'The Wildlife Heritage Foundation at first had no income so we were subsidising the work and the care of the cats there with money from Paradise. That in turn was having the effect of slowing down the development of Paradise.'

To help him run the Smarden site Peter contacted Mark Edgerley, who had previously been in charge of Marwell Zoo, near Winchester. Sadly Mark passed away in 2024. Mark had been involved with zoos for thirty years but had only come into the industry as a full-time professional in 2000. Up until then he had worked outside the industry and as a volunteer and vice-chairman of the board of trustees for Marwell. He had first come across Peter Sampson when Peter was looking for a sponsor to sign his papers when he was applying to become a member of the World Association of Zoos and Aquariums (WAZA). 'That was a very brave move for a small zoo operator in Hertfordshire,' Mark says, 'but I was very happy to back him because I knew what Peter was doing at Paradise, it was very successful and that his heart was in it. It was what I called a very big small zoo because it was big-hearted and delivered a lot, and it had taken a lot of sweat and effort from the Sampson family driven by Peter to get it to the success it had become.

'The zoo world can be very suspicious, and they were of Peter because he was an unknown and he felt in isolation. Because I came into the zoo world late as a full-time professional, although I knew the industry and a lot of people in it,

I could empathise with the feelings and pressure that were inside Peter. He could so easily have said, "Well, if they don't want my help or me to put my effort in and make my contribution to WAZA, then I won't." I didn't want that contribution to be lost so I was very supportive as were others as well and argued that Paradise Wildlife Park was worthy of joining zoo organisations. And of course, it proved more than worthy. I have a lot of respect for Peter. He's done a fantastic job. He's up there with the greats and he has the respect of the zoo world too.'

WAZA membership was achieved, and Mark Edgeley was impressed by Peter's subsequent presence at international zoo meetings in Africa and America, and other worldwide locations, and how he soon became very well known in the zoo fraternity. 'He's such a friendly chap,' Mark says. 'It doesn't matter what nationality you are or what language you speak, he exudes friendliness even if he can't communicate in the lingo.'

After Mark had answered Peter's call to join him in Smarden the two men found their aims, hopes and ambitions were much the same for the site and Mark was duly appointed WHF's chief executive officer. 'Mark's new role was to oversee and manage the site in my absence,' Peter says. 'He carried out this role over many years and was a great asset to the work we undertook at the sanctuary. In Mark's time we established WHF/BCS as a full charity, which in many ways helped us to finance the cats in our care, and the team, as well as support cats in the wild.'

The first trustee was Pete James, a great friend of Peter's who had set up the Santago Rare Leopard Project in Old Welwyn, Hertfordshire. The two Peters had much in common, not just their forenames. They were born just a couple of months apart in 1939 and in their similar post-war upbringing each had displayed an early love of animals.

Committed conservationists both, Pete James had first developed a passion for big cats after his father took him to see the film *Tarzan* at the cinema when he was eleven years old. He eventually obtained a Dangerous Wild Animal licence for the small private collection of leopard species he began assembling in his large rear garden.

Pete lived with his wife Jackie at their home close to woodland near Welwyn Garden City, just 10 miles from Paradise at Broxbourne. Bound by their strong commonly shared passion for big cats, Peter and Rachael became best of friends with Pete and Jackie, their friendship sealed by the former after they generously hosted the couple's wedding at Paradise. Fittingly, Pete and Jackie tied the knot standing on a platform overlooking three lions.

Pete and Jackie treasured Peter's friendship on every level, not least when he answered the occasional emergency call. To Peter's alarm, Pete's big cat enclosures in his garden were in general so rickety that he knew they would invite trouble, and on several occasions, Peter received the call for help in the early hours of the morning. 'Pete's pens were so flimsy I would have kept only chickens in them,' Peter says. 'There were a few times when he called me up in the small hours to ask me to come over quickly as a mesh roof had blown off. I'd hurry over and find myself up on the roof with a broom trying to keep leopards or pumas at bay while Pete tried to re-lay and nail down the mesh. A couple of his cats did escape so there was friction with his neighbours.'

The two Peters, Rachael and Jackie all got on so well that the four of them regularly travelled together to numerous European zoos and wildlife parks to expand their collective understanding and knowledge of caring for big cats. Every zoo was different, every zoo had something new for them all to discover and learn about, and to enjoy.

It was in the mid 1980s that Pete James set up his Santago Rare Leopard Project specialising in clouded leopards, a species on the brink of extinction. Not long afterwards he brought in cats from the US to start breeding and became only the second person in the UK to successfully breed this species of big cat. 'They are hard to breed,' Peter states. 'The males are generally a lot bigger than the females, with the biggest teeth you have ever seen, and Pete's first effort was a disaster. The male killed the female. Pete learned that to breed you have to get them together at a very young age, around twelve to eighteen months, and he became so good at it that I suggested that with his knowledge he should try and become the studbook keeper – which he duly did.'

Peter recalls once taking a nervous trip with Pete over to Belfast to collect a clouded leopard at the height of the Troubles in Northern Ireland. 'There were violent hostilities going on and bombs going off, so for two Englishmen driving through Belfast in a little white van with English number plates it was an exciting but anxious time to say the least. Pete James had no paperwork for the leopard we collected and I was worried as to how we would explain at the border what we had in the crate. We were stopped at the quayside by soldiers bristling with guns, which made me feel very uneasy. When challenged as to what we had in the back of the van and we told them we had a cat in a crate, they thought we were joking and with that we were waved through without even a glance either into the back of the van or into the crate or at any paperwork we might or might not have. That most certainly wouldn't happen today. That trip took three days with no overnight hotel stop and very little sleep. All in all we were glad to get home.'

To help pay for the bills and the upkeep of their cats, Pete and Jackie introduced photographic days, inviting guests to Welwyn with their cameras for the day. Although this was met with much opposition from the neighbours, it proved financially successful and a similar photographic initiative was adopted at WHF/BCS, again with great success. When Pete James continued to face criticism from his neighbours, Peter recommended that he should move to Kent. 'I more or less suggested he should sell up and make a new home near the WHF site at Smarden.'

It was a proposal which Pete and Jackie seriously considered. But not long afterwards on a trip to Barcelona Zoo, both Rachael and Peter noticed that Pete was not his old self. His general health was not good, but he dismissed their worries and the four of them pressed on to Germany and a visit to Berlin Zoo. But soon it became clear his health was seriously deteriorating and he was given the devastating news that he had motor neurone disease, a rare condition affecting the brain and nervous system for which there is no cure.

It took hold very quickly, and Peter and Rachael loyally travelled over to Welwyn to pay him and Jackie a visit at least once a week, often with Dave 'the Otter' Thomas, who was a good friend and long-standing volunteer at Paradise. Dave and other members of the Paradise team also gallantly went to the couple's home to help Jackie care for the leopards. In a bid to ensure his great friend kept in close contact with his beloved clouded leopard collection, Peter went out and bought an electric buggy for him and levelled up much of Pete's garden, and, with the help of WHF trustee Steve Candler, nicknamed 'Steve Tarmac' by Peter after Steve's North Hertfordshire Surfacing company, they laid down pathways in the grounds so he could ride the buggy round to the cat enclosures.

Sadly, Pete's condition deteriorated so quickly that he never had the opportunity to make use of the buggy. He died in 2008, and as a tribute to him Peter built an enclosure for clouded leopards in Pete's name at The Big Cat Sanctuary in Kent. In 2024 a new clouded leopard habitat was built, and since then they have received a female from Howletts Zoo called Boa and a male from Pairi Daiza Zoo in Belgium called Django, who are part of the European Breeding Programme.

After Pete's death, his widow Jackie strove to keep her husband's Santago project alive. But for this she needed to acquire a DWA licence and public liability insurance costing many thousands of pounds. In the end she asked Peter to find homes for her cats. Some went to Paradise, others to The Big Cat Sanctuary. On a positive note for Peter, finding new homes for the animals led him to form a great friendship with Chris Lawton at the Falconry and Owl Sanctuary in Rutland. Peter helped Chris to obtain a DWA licence there which enabled him to launch a Cat Project within his bird sanctuary in tranquil woodland locations which offered a home for cats no longer suitable for breeding programmes. Over the past fifteen years Peter has moved many retiring leopards and pumas to Chris's Rutland operation and helped him financially to care for them.

As work at WHF progressed, much-needed new staff arrived to become valued members of Peter and Mark Edgerley's team. One in particular was Becky, who over time became head cat keeper, along with volunteers, many of whom went on to become paid employees. Peter had a long list of restructure and rebuild projects for the team to tackle, including dismantling much of the old equipment remaining from the Born Free and Marley Farm days including an extremely large incinerator which burned all the waste products. In reality it meant clearing the whole site of what was not required in order to begin afresh, starting with the upgrading and enlarging of the existing enclosures and cat houses.

Initially the WHF/BCS operation afforded Peter the chance to transfer tigers, including Indy, Bruno and Padmini, and his three lion brothers, Tiny, Kafara and Manzi, from Paradise Wildlife Park and to provide a retirement home for others as they aged. But WHF also now gave Peter the space, denied him by the long-established public roads enclosing Paradise, to grasp the opportunity to fulfil his dreams of breeding large endangered cats.

CHAPTER ELEVEN

Well Bred

'I am so proud to be patron of such an incredible organisation'

— *HRH Princess Eugenie*

During the sanctuary's formative years as the Wildlife Heritage Foundation, now The Big Cat Sanctuary (BCS), Peter paved the way to realise his ambitions to breed big cats by talking in earnest to the right people involved with big cats in different parts of the world. He started attending European meetings to make personal contact with various breeding and conservation representatives, including the all-important European Endangered Species Programme (EEP) studbook keepers for a wide range of animals.

In effect Peter had to serve an apprenticeship. He was learning all the time and quickly recognised that breeding is not a simple pick-and-choose procedure. It is a tightly regulated process by the EEP, which makes recommendations for captive breeding in order to produce a strong, healthy and diverse gene pool within the captive population with the ultimate aim of reintroduction into natural habitat to mix with counterparts in the wild.

One EEP committee is dedicated to each species. On each committee is a studbook keeper who keeps detailed genetic data: records of births, deaths, aspects of bloodlines, age, sex and breeding history. Also on the studbook keeper's list will be a global record pinpointing where and when any zoo in the world has held or is holding a particular species. Some records go as far back as the middle of the 19th century, but others have been collated over a period of only the last forty years.

Each committee includes veterinary surgeons, geneticists, people involved with animal husbandry, zoo keepers, conservationists and others who work with species in the wild. They all contribute to bring together a huge volume of knowledge about their species for the EEP committees, which usually meet twice a year. Using this meticulously compiled data on the animals, they are especially anxious to avoid the interbreeding of a father with a daughter or with offspring after one or two litters.

To the casual observer, the work of the EEP is all about breeding. But those involved see it in terms of protecting genetic diversity. It is the genetic lines that are of most importance, a very pure, very scientific sense of breeding. Finally, it is these committees which assess all the applications for breeding and which make all the decisions about who can hold animals for that purpose. It is not easy to win permission from the EEP co-ordinator to breed. Frequently they will advocate only a certain number to be living in captivity, and of course when a matching pair of animals is brought together there is no guarantee they will produce offspring.

Cats generally are difficult to breed and often do not fare well in very busy zoos. They like quiet corners, which is why the WHF/BCS facility was perfect because Peter was adamant from the start that the sanctuary should not be a visitor attraction open all year round to the general public. He wanted any breeding programme he embarked upon to be given the best chance of succeeding without hordes of visitors with differing levels of interest crowding around the animals' enclosures.

It's common knowledge that the world has so many different species of wild animals which are threatened with extinction, but it was Amur leopards which particularly caught Peter's attention as they are the rarest big cats still living in the wild. There are thought to be less than seventy of the species, possibly as few as sixty, living in the forests stretching from the border of China to the Russian coast, the only place on earth where they can be found in the wild. In this part of eastern Russia more people are living there than might be expected and human disturbance of the Amur leopard's habitat in addition to poaching have been responsible for the declining numbers of the species. Economic pressures on the Amurs' forests, including forestry itself, and gas and oil interests all threaten the very existence of the species.

Given the pitifully few surviving numbers, Peter made this highly endangered species his top breeding priority, backed by his good friend and specialist consultant vet John Lewis. With financial help from WHF and Paradise Wildlife Park, John travelled extensively in the Russian far east looking into the plight of Amur leopards and came to realise how desperately close the species was becoming to extinction. He supported Peter's plans to breed, but made him fully aware that even if he was to become a successful breeder, it could be a long time before he would be involved in any re-introduction programme of Amur leopards back into the wild in the Russian far east.

While successful breeding in captivity is considered essential to the long-term survival of the Amur leopard, reintroduction to the wild would need approval from Russian authorities and there would be various administrative procedures to go through before any release could be effected. Animals bred in zoos and wildlife parks cannot simply be let loose for them to run off into their natural habitat. Holding enclosures for the animals would initially need to be built for them to acclimatise to a new future, deer and pigs introduced as prey, and hunters persuaded not to shoot the prey for themselves, nor shoot the animal bred for release.

Additionally, it would not be WHF/BCS's first generation of Amur leopards which would be released into the wild. It would be the second generation, leopards bred in holding enclosures in their rightful habitat and kept in an environment where they would not see keepers too often and where they would regard humans as potential danger. When they in turn produced a litter, they would go into a much larger enclosure with their cubs and have no interaction with people at all, and it's that generation which could go into the wild.

After conducting negotiations with various studbook keepers and talking to committees, Peter put in a request to the co-ordinator of the EEP for WHF to establish a breeding pair of Amur leopards and he was accepted as project leader for the species – a challenging start to WHF's own breeding programme. In preparation, with the help of good friend David Williams, architect at both PWP and WHF, Peter successfully submitted his plans for an Amur leopard breeding complex with a large house and four enclosures to Ashford Council's planning department.

Peter recalls: 'As we were relatively new boys on the block, the studbook keeper started off by first allocating us a male Amur leopard from Cotswold Wildlife Park. Sadly this leopard had no tail so we called him Manx after the famously tail-less cats of the Isle of Man.

'With vet John Lewis in charge, we carried out numerous tests to see if Manx was born with no tail or if his mother had bitten it off at birth. Many different tests took place, including a scan along his backbone to see where the tail may have been. Unfortunately, all of the tests proved negative and as we couldn't be sure, we reluctantly decided that Manx could not be involved in any breeding programme. It was not the start we were looking for.'

In time, the studbook keeper informed Peter there were two Amur leopards in Russia which Peter could hold, provided he could find a way and the money to fund the huge transportation costs to bring them over to England. The UK's relationship with Russia in general has been far from cordial to say the least throughout Peter's lifetime, but he managed to call in a little help from acquaintances at Moscow Zoo, resulting in two leopards, Artur and Artem, duly arriving from Novosibirsk Zoo in the Russian Federation where they were born. But disappointingly, on inspection they both turned out to be male, brothers – not exactly ideal for breeding ambitions.

With Artur and Artem now living happily on site, the search was on for a suitable female. It took three years to find one before a female named Xizi arrived at Smarden from Helsinki Zoo in Finland. Then, Artur and Xizi were moved into the newly built leopard breeding centre but initially kept separate while they became acquainted with each other.

They were finally introduced to one another in the same enclosure four months later and, although Amur leopards are known to be a little feisty, they mated one weekend when Xizi was in season. She became pregnant and, much to Peter's joy, three months later, on Sunday 12 October 2008 at 3 p.m. she produced three cubs. Sadly, the smallest cub died after a few days, but Xizi kept and successfully reared the other two. Two surviving cubs is normal for this species in captivity, whereas it's more common for just a single cub to survive in the wild, where conditions are harsh, food is difficult to come by and there is the constant risk of predators.

The two cubs were named Argun and Anuy after tributaries of the Amur River, known as the Black River or Dragon River, which flows from China through Russia into the Gulf of Amur and the China Sea, and their births came as a very pleasant surprise to the EEP's studbook keeper. Although Xizi was on the list to breed that year, she was not expected to succeed.

There was understandably great excitement and pride among Peter, Mark and the entire WHF team at their remarkable breeding success, made all the more special by the knowledge that Amur leopards were so exceptionally rare and that their two cubs were helping to keep the species alive.

The births of Argun and Anuy rightly earned Peter new respect from the international zoo and breeding world and from the committed global conservation community.

Peter says: 'In many ways breeding any cat can be difficult as they may not be compatible. We've been successful in breeding jaguars, Sumatran tigers, cheetahs, Amur tigers, snow leopards, Pallas's cats and white lions and experience tells me Pallas's cats and clouded leopards are the hardest. I'm really proud of all of our breeding achievements and for me they are all very special. But I feel possibly the most important have been the Amur leopards, bearing in mind they are the rarest cats in the world. What made it even more special the first time was that we had brought the male in as part of the international breeding programme from northern Russia.'

While the breeding of Amur leopard cubs was widely recognised as a great accomplishment, Peter and his team managed another rare feat that same year, by successfully breeding Sumatran tigers – and once more against all the odds. As with most large predators, the Sumatran tiger is suffering loss of habitat due to increased human use of the areas where they are found, with fewer than 400 surviving in the wild. Every week another Sumatran tiger in the wild is killed by poachers, and rapid forest destruction and replacement with monoculture oil palm plantations are threatening the Sumatran tiger's extinction.

Peter had acquired a parent-reared male Sumatran tiger from Berlin Zoo, and a hand-reared female from Heidelberg Zoo. The tigress had never reared a cub of her own before and proved to be a small, nervous cat. But thanks to the animal husbandry techniques Peter was developing at WHF and the way he kept the cats calm, cool and quiet, Sumatran tiger cubs duly arrived. Again this was a doubly unexpected success given that it was unusual in the zoo world for a hand-reared female to rear a first litter.

Mark Edgerley commented: 'It's testament to the respect Peter has in the industry that both the Amur leopards and the Sumatran tigers we were given were top ranking in the breeding list of endangered animals. When he arrived, the Sumatran tiger male was number two in the top fifty males in the breeding programme in Europe. The only Sumatran male tiger ranked more important than him in the whole of Europe was the father of the female they sent us from Heidelberg. They were the top two lines together.'

The importance of the arrival of WHF's thoroughbred Sumatran tiger cubs, Bawa and Asu, both males, should not be overestimated. Like the Amur leopard, the species will only survive with captive breeding.

After five years of hard work in expanding and restructuring Marley Farm, Peter felt justified in staging the very first WHF Open Day, partly to dispel annoyingly unfounded rumours which had begun to spread that the WHF was secretly a station for animal experiments. The fact that the public had never been given access to the site had begun to arouse suspicions. Peter organised for leaflets to be dropped round to local residents announcing the WHF would be open to visitors for just one day between the hours of 3 p.m. to 7 p.m., specifically timed so that those at work had a chance to visit.

Around seventy inquisitive local residents attended plus others from the nearby industrial estate, and they were welcomed with jugs of orange juice served from crisp white tablecloths on two long tables before being given a guided tour. The visitors departed not only reassured there were no animal experiments being conducted, but mostly amazed, supportive and full of respect for what the WHF was endeavouring to do for conservation and what it had already achieved in a few short years.

The success of that first open day paved the way for what has now become a hugely popular handful of days each year when BCS opens its heavy electric security gates to the public to see for themselves some of the rarest cats on the planet. The open days currently attract many thousands to BCS and they have become so popular that it has become necessary to allow entry by pre-booked tickets. The whole site takes on an atmosphere of a country fair and offers a great opportunity for BCS members to visit and see the cats in its care. The money raised from the open days goes towards the running of BCS as well as to conservation work.

Since the arrival of Amur leopard and Sumatran tiger cubs, Peter's record as a breeder of endangered big cats at BCS has been remarkable and now encompasses snow leopards, Amur tigers, rarely-seen-in-the-wild Pallas's cats and jaguars. His breeding successes have come with the help and guidance of head keeper Becky Hall, curator Briony Smith, deputy head keeper Ricky Reino and their respective teams.

Once Peter had the WHF/BCS up and running so efficiently, expansion rapidly increased. The more Ashford Council grasped Peter's passion for the cats in his care and his commitment to conservation, the more amenable the council became to his building plans to develop the site. Two major steps forward were the granting of planning permission to construct a large timber building called Heritage Lodge and the agreement for a re-routing of the sanctuary's main entrance.

Heritage Lodge, comprising reception desks, two large guest lounges, a kitchen and toilet facilities, was designed as a visitor centre for guests and BCS members and it complemented a newly created driveway entrance. From the start Peter had been unhappy about the original entry into the site which necessitated driving through an old industrial site. He felt that it was an unwelcoming approach to an animal sanctuary. Instead, solidly secure, heavy electronic gates were erected in front of a long driveway leading to a car park close to Heritage Lodge.

More negotiations with Malcolm Dudding eventually enabled Peter to purchase a further eight acres of land adjoining the site. This took the total to 32 acres, matching the land area at Paradise at that time. Again with planning consent, the extra land allowed for the building of larger enclosures with improved landscaping for the lions and tigers in the sanctuary's care and for the extension of all four of the enclosures around the Amur leopard complex. The extra space was of great benefit to the cats as it gave them more room to exercise and climb.

Peter was adamant from the start of his operation that the health of every animal was monitored closely, even to the extent of setting aside dentist days at BCS for examination of his cats' teeth. Even big cats need a tooth capped every once in a while.

He was prepared to arrange treatment for any animal which became unwell, and in the spring of 2009, emergency procedures were suddenly called for when Tiny, one of the sanctuary's standout lions in the sanctuary's twenty-five-year history, became very sick for a few days. Tests showed that Tiny had developed a problem when he was being weaned. The valve at the pit of his stomach had not formed properly so he was unable to pass meat through into his intestines. Peter was aware of this potential weakness and it manifested itself much later on when the lion picked up too much hair off his food – horse meat, which has a certain amount of skin and horse hair in it because it helps with digestion. Tiny was also found to have three fur balls in his intestines and a lump of fur stuck in the valve causing projectile vomiting.

Peter was within hours of losing the lion, but he is renowned for always finding the money for a vet bill and he gathered a large veterinary team together and Tiny was transported off to a veterinary surgery in Maidstone for an emergency operation. But they were not aware what an incredible fighter Tiny was and what strength of character he had. Not only did he survive his illness, but he went on to outlive his two brothers.

'All three grew from young boys into handsome lions in their prime,' Peter recalls. 'They arrived from Paradise Wildlife Park as two-year-olds, just teenagers by lion standards, and all three of them living together made a wonderful spectacle for everyone to see, especially when lying lined up side by side on their platform.

'Tiny could be distinguished from his brothers by his huge mane, his broad, square-shaped muzzle and his almost perfect unscarred face, a rarity for a lion living with others. Normally nicks and scratches are evidence of a life lived together in a group. True to form, however, Tiny would start mischief and then get out of the way while his brothers play-tussled, allowing his ego as well as his face to remain pristine.'

Inevitably age eventually caught up with Tiny when he was eighteen and a half years old. Through close monitoring it became apparent he was slowing down. His joints had become stiff and his balance was becoming unsteady. 'A decision was taken to try a new medication on him to see if his condition improved,' Peter says, 'but sadly it did not have the necessary effect, and we were unable to keep his joint condition under control. With a very heavy heart it was time to say goodbye to our Tiny.

'It is never easy to say goodbye to any of our cats, let alone ones that have been with us for a long time. Dear Tiny will never be forgotten. His time at The Big Cat Sanctuary will always be a part of the sanctuary's original foundations. The passing of Tiny and his brothers was like an end of an era for us at the sanctuary. The trio had resided with us for seventeen years and had proved to be great ambassadors for not only the lions of Africa but for the WHF/BCS itself.'

The necessity to transport Tiny all the way to Maidstone for his hairball removal operation was one of the reasons that in time prompted Peter to build an Animal Resource Centre (ARC) on site at BCS: a state-of-the-art facility with veterinary rooms and a dedicated veterinary hospital complete with an observation room, allowing students to view through a reinforced glass window the operations on big cats as they take place. Plans for the ARC included provision of rooms to study and each year BCS hosts three or more post-graduate students to work and learn for a twelve-month period of internship.

The ARC was the largest project Peter had undertaken since BCS was launched. To help with the construction Peter was fortunate to have the assistance of a team of Gurkhas based at Maidstone and the soldiers were on site for four weeks undertaking timber work. It was the second time Peter had enlisted the assistance of Gurkhas, as they had contributed once before to the building of BCS's largest enclosure for white lions. 'Everything we do has got bigger and better for the welfare of the cats,' Peter says. 'We've brought in heated mats for the cats to lie on, introduced heating in their houses, full insulation, more space, more climbing frames, more activities and the veterinary care is as good as we can get it.'

Keeping pace with all the construction projects at the sanctuary throughout the years of its existence have been new births and the arrival of new cats and new species, with tigers all the while remaining Peter's particular passion. Apart from Tiny and his brothers, several cats that were transferred from Paradise, including an Amur tiger and a puma, other big cat arrivals at BCS have come from abroad: an Amur leopard from Helsinki, a Sumatran tiger from Heidelberg Zoo in Germany, an Amur tiger from Schwerin, and a fishing cat from Leipzig. Newcomers have also included two north Chinese leopards, one from France and one from Berlin, while other animals including leopards and ocelots have arrived from a range of wildlife parks and zoos.

Each new arrival has been different – and sometimes unpredictable. 'We had a tiger come in from Germany and it was the wildest thing I've ever seen,' Peter recalls. 'It was paranoid about people. One moment it would run at the fence and charge at you, the next it would run and hide under a bush.'

As we have seen, there is a willingness to help each other in the zoo and wildlife park fraternity, and on one occasion Peter took in an elderly female jaguar from Chester Zoo so as to allow the Chester team to bring in a new bloodline. Also, to help London Zoo, he took in two elderly Sumatran tigers, Riker and Lumper, which gave London Zoo the opportunity to bring in a younger breeding pair.

Every successful breeding at BCS has naturally been greeted by Peter and his team with much excitement, satisfaction, pleasure and immense pride. New arrivals and transfers from Paradise have been afforded an equally warm welcome, not least the rare Pallas's cats after the birth of four kittens, all strong and healthy. The very first kittens were born at Paradise, before they moved to WHF/BCS.

It was always Peter's intention to breed endangered big cats for the international breeding programme, never for self-gratification nor for personal glory, nor simply as an ostentatious triumph for BCS. 'I've always been happy to move our offspring far and wide,' he emphasises, 'and we considered it a great achievement when, for example, a female Amur leopard went off to America to Hogle Zoo in Salt Lake City, and two fishing cats were relocated, one to France and another to Prague in the Czech Republic, as part of the EEP international breeding programme. We also transferred one of our Amur leopard cubs to Hiroshima in Japan as part of the global breeding programme. It's important for BCS to play a part in helping other wildlife parks and zoos with their own breeding programmes.'

Together with his successes in breeding, Peter has demonstrated a willingness to explore and develop new handling techniques for his big cats. When building new enclosures, he has strived to provide mounds and platforms that are more challenging for the cats to climb and outside shelters, while ensuring there are logs and bark for claw scratching. He has also introduced heated mats and rocks, and pools for the tigers and jaguars, plus meat hanging on clips for cats to pounce upon as they would in the wild.

One year, when violent winter storms caused extensive damage at the sanctuary's tiger complex, Peter decided with the support of the trustees to carry out a complete rebuild of all four tiger enclosures in the complex. The originals had been constructed with large round timber posts but these were now replaced with heavy-duty box steel posts. The alterations, undertaken by Terry Hall and the buildings team, also presented an opportunity to improve the landscaping with new ponds and to make each enclosure slightly bigger. It proved to be an extremely large project which took two years from start to finish. On completion Peter was satisfied that the complex was not only considerably stronger but a much safer environment for the tigers in his care.

Work had not gone very far when in 2020 Covid hit the UK. This slowed the construction of the ARC considerably, and it was a long way from completion when Peter suffered two very personal blows. His long-established chief vet John Lewis died unexpectedly, and not long afterwards his architect David Williams fell ill with Covid and died in hospital within a week.

Peter was shocked and deeply saddened at their deaths. He counted the two men as very close friends and each in their very different ways over a long period of time had contributed so much to the success of both Paradise Wildlife Park and The Big Cat Sanctuary.

'I felt the wind had been taken out of my sails,' he says, 'and I said openly that without John I would give up on the ARC project. But after a week or two and after long talks with Lynn and other members of my family, and with our sanctuary team as well as with John and David's wives, we all agreed it would be an opportunity to build something in their names. The ARC project could take off again, but more so in their memory.'

John Lewis's passing was especially sad for BCS because he had agreed to take up Peter's offer for him to head up the veterinary operation at the ARC. His acceptance was one of the chief reasons Peter was keen to build the ARC in the first place, as he explains: 'John had stated he wanted his life to slow down, to reduce the amount of time he spent travelling and to cut back on his extremely large vet practice. I'd told him that if we could obtain planning permission for this new building to include a dedicated veterinary hospital with a classroom for students to study, he could base himself at the sanctuary. By concentrating on that, it would greatly reduce his overall workload. John's exact words to me were: "Yes, let's go for it."'

It was in 2018 that the WHF was renamed The Big Cat Sanctuary, still remaining a full charity (1104420). It has flourished and developed into an incredible success story through Peter, his family, the team and trustees' dedicated governance and has earned an enviable record for breeding, for funding conservation initiatives around the world and for providing a safe haven for some of the world's most endangered cats.

Over the past twenty-five years, BCS has expanded beyond recognition, with larger enclosures housing a wider variety of cat species. Along with success as a breeding centre, meeting conservation objectives, it has put finances back into the local economy – similarly with Paradise, now Hertfordshire Zoo.

More recent BCS successes in the Endangered Species Breeding Programme include the birth of a rare black jaguar, Inka, in April 2021. Then

July 2023 saw the arrival of two snow leopard cubs, a third successful litter born to Laila, who willingly underwent an ultrasound scan which enabled BCS to prepare for their arrival. The breeding of two new snow leopard cubs was rightly acclaimed by conservationists worldwide as hugely significant.

* * *

When Cheryl and Neville Williams and Jon Minion, the trio who for many years had been the driving force behind Woburn Safari Park, decided to set up their own wildlife park with their own financial backing, Peter was only too happy to help.

The trio had purchased a large location on the outskirts of Doncaster. A highlight of their plans was for an extremely large lion house, and an even larger enclosure with a view to bringing in a big pride of lions from Eastern Europe from a zoo which had closed down. Since BCS was a big cat charity, Peter was asked to help raise funds to finance the building of the enclosure and to help pay for transporting the lions.

With the help of son Steve, Peter set up a fundraising account at BCS in conjunction with a national newspaper, which raised the impressive amount of £150,000 for the trio's new lion project. It was another proud moment for Peter when he was invited to hand over the cheque to Yorkshire Wildlife Park. Since then, the park has flourished and has become a thriving success.

* * *

For all of the early years of its existence, the sanctuary – in common with other zoos and wildlife parks – was forbidden to hold African lions and Asian lions together on the same site or at the same location. It was thought by veterinary experts that African lions carried a form of bacteria which, if spread to Asian lions, could possibly kill them. But after many years of research, it was proved that this is not the case. So, when BCS received the news that Bristol Zoo was closing and relocating to a new site, Peter was legitimately allocated the zoo's pair of Asiatic lions. The lions arrived after months of negotiations with the zoo and the studbook keeper. There are very few Asiatic lions in zoos and wildlife parks worldwide and they are part of the international breeding programme. So the arrival of the two lions named Sonika and Sahee thus made BCS almost certainly the only location in the UK, and most probably the only one in Europe, that holds both species of lion.

BCS today is unrecognisable in every way from the Marley Farm Peter bought twenty-five years ago. As years went by, WHF/BCS became financially able to pay its own way rather than relying on funding from Paradise and this was partly due to the successful open days and rising BCS membership numbers as well as the chance to book overnight stays at the sanctuary in one of eight luxury lodges specifically constructed by Peter's long-term colleague Vic Cooper. A number of big cat experiences have been introduced to help cover the running costs of BCS. They include photographic workshops, big cat encounters and an opportunity to become a ranger for the day, assisting and shadowing a keeper. There is also the chance to feed big cats, part of a regular routine to bring cats close to keepers to allow them the best opportunity to spot any developing health issues.

All these initiatives help support the sanctuary's proclaimed five pillars of ethos: Welfare, Breeding, Education, Conservation and Rescue, the latter being added in 2024/25 due to the Big Cats in Crisis project to bring in five lions from war-torn Ukraine suffering from shell shock and from the illegal wildlife trade.

Monthly donations provide essential funds to care for the cats, including food, veterinary care and habitat maintenance as well as multiple conservation efforts around the world. Cat adoption and sponsorship schemes also add to paying the cost of vet and food bills.

Together with family, team members and trustees, Peter laid the foundations for making WHF/BCS the very successful breeding centre that it is today and, in 2018, awareness of and interest in the sanctuary and its conservation work globally received an enormous boost thanks to a TV documentary miniseries called *Big Cats About the House*. It featured the work of conservationist Giles Clark at BCS and in particular his hand-raising of a very small and delicate female black jaguar cub called Maya at his home. Maya had arrived at the sanctuary at five days old from Wingham Wildlife Park in Kent after effectively being rejected by her mother who could neither provide her with adequate milk nor care. It was felt that the baby jaguar stood the best chance of survival if she was hand-reared by Giles.

Giles had started out working with big cats with Peter at Paradise when he was a teenager, before subsequently leaving the UK to settle in Australia, where he became Head of Tigers and Conservation at Australia Zoo in Queensland. When he returned to work with Peter as Director of Cats and Conservation at BCS, Giles proved not only a natural on television but hugely popular with viewers too.

Big Cats About the House became a massive hit with audiences of all ages and especially with younger viewers. The TV series originally intended to follow Maya growing up but it took on added value for viewers with the unexpected additional arrival at BCS from Wingham Wildlife Park of a female cheetah cub called Willow. As one of three cubs in a litter, Willow had been rejected by her two brothers at Wingham and it was felt, as with Maya, that her best chance of survival would be in the care of Giles and BCS. The TV cameras were thus able to capture Giles and his wife Kathryn raising not one but two very different cats in Maya and Willow. The TV crew followed their stories as the cubs grew bigger and stronger every day, with the help from Peter, BCS curator Briony Smith, deputy head keeper Ricky Reino and the team.

The series following the growing cubs went out on BBC2 and also followed Giles on his conservation travels abroad on behalf of BCS. In Kenya he was featured fitting BCS-donated collars on lions to help rangers keep track of them, partly to keep them safe from poachers but also for rangers to steer them away from villages as they roamed.

Filming of Giles's further conservation work abroad followed him to Cambodia raising funds for wild cats, seeing one of the most important rainforest corridors in Central America, and planting hundreds of donated young trees in Costa Rica.

In that same year, 2018, the sanctuary was given prestigious royal backing when, after a meeting of trustees with HRH Princess Eugenie at Buckingham Palace, she agreed to become a BCS patron. Shortly afterwards Peter was able to show the princess around the site and she was able to take up his offer to feed one of the big cats.

Princess Eugenie has proved a worthy patron. She invited BCS trustees and their guests to a special reception she hosted at St James's Palace, and in 2018 Peter and Rachael and BCS chairman Sir Eric Peacock and his wife Carol were invited to her wedding to Jack Brooksbank.

Princess Eugenie became a patron at a time when a jaguar breeding centre was being built at BCS incorporating a large enclosure to the front with landscaping, tree planting, climbing platforms and a pool plus a large dedicated and insulated house in the middle with several internal pens with heated platforms and a keeper area. Another large landscaped enclosure was built to the rear with climbing areas and pool to be utilised if breeding was successful.

Once the complex was completed, Princess Eugenie helped BCS celebrate its twentieth anniversary in style by officially opening the Jaguar Breeding Centre in 2020 by declaring: 'I am so proud to be patron of such an incredible organisation.'

CHAPTER TWELVE

'A white lion pride at Paradise Wildlife Park was a notable first'

— *Peter Sampson*

The more Paradise flourished, the wider were Peter's ambitions. He considered the possibility of adding white lions as an exceptional feature of Paradise, as they were very rarely seen in the UK. There was only one other wildlife park in the country where this extremely rare and beautiful variant of a lion was to be found.

In preparation Peter began getting in touch with friends in South Africa who in turn had contacts with keepers of white lions. He gleaned enough information and made such promising connections that he was able to fly to Johannesburg to embark on what he calls his white lion adventure, his search for the very rare species.

He says: 'I discovered that they were found mainly in the wilds of South Africa in a region called Timbavati. This was an area thought to have been home for centuries to the white lion although the earliest recorded sighting in this region was only in 1938. It is there that lions can carry a recessive gene which causes a rare colour mutation by which a naturally brown female lion can have three cubs, one brown, one biscuit colour and one white cub. Sadly, over time, the numbers of white lions in the wild had dwindled due to the poaching and stealing of young cubs. Equally sadly, game hunters had paid huge sums of money to shoot adult male white lions.'

Peter was accompanied on his journey to South Africa by Chris Van Schalkwyk, one of the Paradise team who was South African by birth and knew his way around his mother country. Together with Chalkie, as Chris was known to one and all, Peter travelled to various locations in South Africa looking for the elusive white lions. Whenever their search was successful there was jubilation but there was disappointment too from a breeding point of view. Too many of the white lions they came across had been interbred, leaving them with a range of defects and health issues.

Finally, they headed by light aircraft to Kimberley, where they were met at the airport by a member of the family whom they had pre-planned to visit, before making their way to stay on their ranch on a massive game reserve which stretched to thousands of acres.

'There we had the opportunity to meet the ranch owner, Wiets Botes,' Peter says. 'He was a real gentleman who had a vast knowledge of African wildlife. Most importantly for me, he had a pride of white lions which were his passion, and we were able to spend many hours discussing the possibility of us purchasing a pair of them from his pride.

'A major part of his land was the game reserve and the ranch itself was home to a large herd of hoofstock including zebra, wildebeest and many more. It transpired that some of the people who came to stay were there to shoot hoofstock, sadly not with a camera but with a gun. They were marksmen and -women from the US and Germany, there to shoot zebra and wildebeest. It was well organised and well managed by the guides, but I did tell Wiets I felt unhappy about this. He replied by asking for the chance to explain.'

Wiets told Peter that each year he and his team culled or shot thirty or more of his ill, weak or aged hoofstock and that each year thirty or more are born. The reality was that he could not hold or sustain the extra animal numbers, and he selected only the old and weak animals for the cull. This, he stressed, created jobs and work for twenty-five local people from the nearby villages and the meat from those kills went straight to the villagers. The truth was that it was the money from these guests from the US and Germany that financed the whole operation.

'I started to feel more at ease,' Peter says. 'Then he pointed out that we carry out much the same procedure in the UK with the shooting of deer in the Scottish Highlands and the shooting of pheasant and partridges. He also pointed out to me that we in the UK also kill cattle, pigs and sheep for meat.

'I ended up having to agree with him. But he totally assured me that he would never, ever allow a single white lion to be shot.'

The rancher then gave Peter the opportunity to take a good look among his pride of white lions with a view to selecting a young female and a slightly older male to take back to the UK. Peter chose a fully grown, majestic, powerful male called Thabo and a young white female called Nala. Negotiations began in earnest.

The purchase price of £20,000 per lion and the cost of transporting the pair proved to be extremely expensive, but Peter had already purpose-built a first-class house and enclosure to prepare for the arrival of white lions and there was no turning back.

'It was a very special day when they eventually arrived at Paradise,' he recalls warmly. 'Everyone was very excited to see such magnificent rare big cats. We had to quarantine them for a while, but once that period was over, they proved to be a great attraction for our visitors and guests, some of whom were happy to travel very long distances just to see our rare new arrivals.'

Both lions settled well into their new environment and Peter was immensely proud of them, venturing into the house of the young lioness, Nala, to sit with her every day along with other members of the Paradise keeper team. 'Nala was the most fantastic young lioness,' Peter effuses, 'and Thabo, the white male, was a beautiful, fully grown, very powerful, majestic lion. After several months Wiets came to visit us from South Africa and said how impressed he was with their new house and enclosure, and with the condition of the lions.'

Time passed uneventfully until out of the blue it became apparent that Nala was experiencing problems with walking. She was well on the way to adulthood, but she was clearly finding it difficult to walk. Alarmingly, she became a pitiful sight, dragging her rear legs behind her as she tried to move forward.

Vet John Lewis checked her over, and it was agreed that Nala should go to the Royal Veterinary College for X-rays and various tests to discover the problem and to find a way to treat it. A full day at the college was set aside for wide-ranging tests and hugely expensive scans.

The results of the scans were devastating. 'They showed Nala was suffering from skeletal deformities,' Peter explains. 'By now she was eighteen months old, well on the way to being fully grown, but as she had grown her backbone had become badly twisted. It had started to arch and was pressing on her spinal cord, which in turn affected the functioning of her rear legs. The stark diagnosis was that basically the vertebrae in her back were crushing her spinal cord thereby causing paralysis in her hind quarters. It was felt that this could have been a birth defect.

'Her situation was deteriorating, and I was worried that she was in great pain,' says Peter. 'I had more meetings with John Lewis, Lynn, and our team of keepers and in the end as a team we had to make the devastating decision to put her to sleep. I can honestly say it was one of the saddest days for me and the whole team. Everyone was sobbing. We had lost our beautiful princess Nala. It was a devastating day.'

It took Peter many months to get over the shock of losing Nala. But as time went by, he took the decision to travel back to Kimberley to meet up again with rancher Wiets with a view to acquiring more white lions. This time he travelled with Paradise colleague Dave 'the Otter' Thomas and they were able to select another two young females, one biscuit coloured and the other white.

'As before we made all the travel arrangements, worked out the finances and a few weeks later the two young lionesses arrived at Paradise. As before, a period of quarantine followed before they were settled in with Thabo. As the months passed by, we were treated to the arrival of our first litter of white lion cubs.'

The cubs were assured of a great welcome. Given all the time, travel, effort, expense and the sadness surrounding the unexpected demise months earlier of Nala, their arrival was greeted with immense joy and satisfaction by everyone, not least by Peter. He had his own white lion pride at Paradise Wildlife Park. 'It was a notable first,' he says.

'We then made the decision to have a pride of white lions at The Big Cat Sanctuary. We set about building the largest house and enclosure that we have ever built with the team at the sanctuary, but also with the help of the Gurkha regiment from Maidstone. Once this large new facility was completed we ventured once more to South Africa to see Wiets in Kimberley, bringing back two female lionesses. By then we had the opportunity to move one of our young males from Paradise. In the coming months we were extremely pleased to welcome two litters of cubs, making the pride complete.'

White lion litters were subsequently born at BCS, where the first litter produced four cubs, with the team heartened by the fact that all four were being happily reared by their mother. Although the cubs were fit and well, Peter or members of his team endeavoured to go into their enclosure every few days to check over the young cubs and weigh them, while making sure their mother was safely in a different part of the enclosure. Only a few weeks after the arrival of this first litter, the second litter of two more cubs arrived and, like the first, they were mother-reared and proved to be strong and healthy.

Sadly, at Paradise Thabo passed away suddenly at an early age but Peter was fortunate to bring in another male, Moto, from West Midlands Safari Park. At Paradise, Peter and the team built a white lion complex called Lion Pride Lands to replace what he had built for his original Broxbourne Zoo lion, Bobby. This comprised an extremely big house and two very large paddocks with heated rocks and a timber viewing building with full-length glass windows so guests and visitors could have a clear view of his very special lions. The new house included heated dens with off-show dens for the welfare of the cats.

Many years after building the first large white lion complex at The Big Cat Sanctuary, it was decided by the trustees to build a new habitat for them at the far side of the sanctuary, which opened in 2024. Peter had decided that the enclosure he had already built for his BCS white lions needed to be replaced and work began on dismantling and clearing away the smaller side of the complex before plans were drawn up along with the trustees to set aside a budget and a two-year timetable for the construction of a brand-new enclosure, aiming to be four times bigger than the original, with a new house with all modern facilities, including full insulation, a heated floor for the winter months as well as solar panels for the roof.

In 2024 Peter and the Paradise team were sad to lose Kya, an adult white lioness Peter had picked out at Wiets Safari sixteen years earlier. 'We had been extremely fortunate that Kya did produce cubs,' Peter reflected. 'It's always a sad loss but she reached a very good age of seventeen years. We also lost Moto, such an iconic, magical lion, at the age of seventeen, which was again a huge loss to us all.'

White lions continue to thrive at The Big Cat Sanctuary, and the Hertfordshire white lionesses Izula and Zuri moved to BCS to be with Kasanga in early 2025, to make way for the habitat to be refurbished ready for the Asiatic lions, Sonika and Sahee, to arrive for Easter 2025 from BCS. But Kya and Moto's passing has been a reminder of how precious the species is. Because, sadly, when Peter's while lions die out, he will be forbidden to replace them. A directive from BIAZA and EAZA, his zoo associations, has ruled that there is no conservation value in keeping either white lions or white tigers – a huge disappointment for Peter.

**

Thanks to his owning a van fully equipped and spacious enough to transport large cats, Peter became much in demand within the zoo world in the UK for his willingness to help move animals around upon request. Unselfishly and generously he was prepared to do so without payment.

Looking back down the years on his travels collecting or transporting big cats, several inevitably stand out, and the day he became the only man ever to deliver a white lion to the Isle of Wight is one. Accompanied by colleague Brian Badger, Peter's day began by travelling to West Midlands Safari Park in Bewdley, Worcestershire, in hazardous, snowy and wintery conditions. As was common on such trips, it required an early start from Paradise, this time at 4 a.m., for a drive through thick snow to the West Midlands Safari Park to collect a fully grown white male African lion. No sooner was the lion safely loaded than the weather took another turn for the worse. The snow very quickly became thicker still, and a tractor was required to tow the van and its precious cargo off the park, before starting a journey of 166 miles to Southampton to board the Isle of Wight ferry.

On arrival in the Isle of Wight, Peter and Brian found the conditions just as bad. 'As we drove across the island, we found many roads closed because of the snow and ice,' Peter remembers. 'Local residents said they had never seen worse conditions on the roads. However, we did manage to settle the lion in at the Isle of Wight Zoo with director Charlotte Corney, then set off on the return journey by ferry and snowy roads again, arriving back at Paradise just before midnight. A very interesting but a very long and tiring day.'

Another journey Peter remembers was answering a call to rescue two very elderly leopards from a wildlife park in Cricket Saint Thomas in Somerset, best known at the time as a filming location for the hit TV series *To the Manor Born*. The park was closing down, and Peter volunteered to set off on the 166-mile road trip in his van to the park situated in the depths of the West Country to collect a pair of leopards, helped again by Brian Badger.

That entailed setting off at 6 a.m. for the long journey to Somerset to load up the cats, then setting off again for another four-hour journey of 216 miles to deliver the leopards to their new home at Chris Lawton's Rutland Wildlife Sanctuary.

By the time Peter reached Rutland a blizzard was blowing, the roads and fields were covered in snow and the night was pitch black. 'Unloading the two leopards and placing them in their new enclosure in the dark wasn't easy,' he says with a grin. 'And we still had to make another journey of 86 miles back to Paradise, arriving just before midnight.'

Always willing to travel far and wide, Peter was approached by another good friend, Anthony Bush, at Noah's Ark Farm and Zoo in Somerset, asking if he would transfer three young lions to him from yet another firm friend, Kim Simmons, at Linton Zoo in Cambridge. Clocking up the miles made for tiring days, but it never seemed to dull Peter's enthusiasm for helping with transportation of cats with the aid of colleagues Steve Saunders and Brian Badger.

CHAPTER THIRTEEN

Cheetahs

'It's still a mystery how we were left empty-handed'
— *Peter Sampson*

Not every attempt to breed has always gone entirely to plan. Peter's ambition to hold cheetahs at Paradise as part of the EEP breeding programme initially proved to be a long, drawn out, difficult and ultimately most frustrating venture.

Right from the early days of Paradise, Peter developed a friendship with Hanika Laumann, generally acknowledged as Europe's leading expert in the breeding and rearing of cheetahs. Hanika was based in the Netherlands and Peter paid a visit to her and her husband Jan on several occasions to learn more about keeping cheetahs. Hanika had cheetah contacts all over the world and she was confident she could find Peter a pair for Paradise.

In preparation, Peter set about building with Hanika's advice a dedicated enclosure and house for cheetahs at Paradise and carried out the necessary work on his van to convert it into a vehicle suitable for transporting cats. Once the enclosure and van had been inspected and approved by the local authority, Hanika arranged for Peter and Rachael to travel with her to Dvůr Králové Safari Park in the Czech Republic, noted for holding cheetahs.

There Peter met up with the park's operators and keepers and he showed them photographs of the specially prepared cheetah enclosure he had built at Paradise. He was anxious to reassure them that Paradise was ready and fully equipped to care for any cheetahs they were prepared to part with.

Once everyone was satisfied with Paradise's credentials, Peter and Rachael were escorted into a large enclosure containing seven cheetahs, all male, whereupon Rachael dropped to one knee to take some photographs. 'Suddenly she was surrounded by all seven of the cats,' Peter remembers, 'and we had to carry out a quick rescue.' It was only a slight scare, nothing more, and if anything, it strengthened Peter's and Rachael's interest in buying a pair for breeding at Paradise.

Agreement was reached for the purchase of two of the cats at a cost of several thousand pounds, but disappointingly for Peter's breeding plans they were both male. Peter consoled himself that at least he would have cheetahs at Paradise and in time he could acquire a female. He then set about applying for the permit and paperwork required to import the two cats from abroad.

The day came when the two cheetahs were flown into Heathrow, with Peter and head keeper Colin Elcombe at the airport ready to collect them in the large, specially kitted out van. They took with them what they believed to be the correct paperwork, a copy of the certificate allowing for them to receive the two cats from the Czech Republic in accordance with the terms laid down in the Convention on International Trade in Endangered Species (CITES). This was a multilateral treaty signed in 1975 to ensure any international animal trade does not threaten the survival of the species in the wild.

To their annoyance and frustration, the authorities at Heathrow would not accept the CITES permit as it was only a photocopy. Peter was shocked. He says: 'Although the permit and its terms were all there in black and white for everyone to see, they insisted on seeing the original document.'

To obtain the original permit, Peter immediately got in touch with the UK office of CITES based in Bristol and made an appointment for the following morning. Next day he and Colin rose early and were ready at 4.30 a.m. to drive to Bristol to obtain the original permit in person. With the two cheetahs incarcerated at Heathrow, they were so anxious to have the matter sorted out quickly that they arrived at the relevant office well before it opened up its doors.

Eventually Peter was able to make clear to a CITES official, whose name is not to be mentioned but remains embedded in Peter's brain, the reason for his visit and why he was in such a hurry. 'I explained that all our paperwork was in good order and that the licensing people had inspected and approved our new enclosure and house for the cheetahs and even the van that we had travelled in. All we wanted was the original permit which we had never been given so we could return to Heathrow to pick up our cheetahs. But the CITES official informed us that the legal department would have to be consulted first.

'I couldn't understand, and still can't, why he needed to check with the legal department,' Peter says. 'It was bureaucracy at its worst and we left empty-handed, totally disappointed and having got no further forward. Worse, the matter stayed unresolved for six weeks of frustrating phone calls and all the while our cheetahs were stuck at Heathrow in very poor conditions.'

Even more frustratingly for Peter, his bid to take the cheetahs to Paradise ended only when the two cats were mystifyingly handed over into the care of Paignton Zoo in Devon.

'To me, this was devastating,' Peter says. 'I couldn't understand the reasoning behind this whatsoever and I still don't know the true facts. I had bought the cheetahs, paid for their transport by air to the UK, and I had invested a great deal of time and expense in building their enclosure and kitting out the van. So how did it come about that Paignton Zoo had received our two cheetahs? And without any preparation or paperwork?

'When I contacted Paignton Zoo, they offered to cover our costs, but I refused their offer saying they would always be our cheetahs. I then had the difficult job of trying to explain what had happened to Hanika in the Netherlands and our new friends in the Czech Republic. Their reactions were unprintable. Interestingly, although Paignton brought in female cheetahs for the two males, they didn't successfully breed at that time.'

Eventually Peter did receive a cheetah from Colchester Zoo in Essex and another from Marwell Zoo near Winchester and they went on to produce two litters. Even then Peter's cheetah problems were not over. 'Sadly, several of the cubs had distorted front legs,' he says. 'Vet John Lewis arranged for them to have scans at the Royal Veterinary College at Potters Bar and the scans showed they needed to have operations to straighten out their front legs. Happily, the ops were a success.'

Peter then went on to build a new cheetah facility at The Big Cat Sanctuary, and in contact with the cheetah studbook keeper Lars Versteege, he was asked to contact Sean Mckeown at Fota Wildlife Park in Cork, Ireland. Peter decided to travel by road and ferry, and was accompanied by his good friend Dave the Otter. They travelled by ferry from north Wales across to Dublin, then drove through southern Ireland to Cork with an overnight stay. 'The following morning we met with our good friend Shaun and we were allocated a male cheetah, which I named Murphy, after Ireland and a good friend, Alan Murphy.

'Once we had loaded Murphy into our van, we made our way to the docks to take an overnight ferry from Cork to Plymouth. But just as we were about to load the van on to the ferry, we were stopped by a customs official who asked me to open the back door so he could have a look inside, which I did. He then asked what was in the crate. When I told him it was a cheetah, he asked, "Is it alive?" I replied, "I ******* hope so!" Then, with a roar of laughter, we shut the door and carried on boarding the ferry for our overnight journey. After docking in Plymouth we made our way back to The Big Cat Sanctuary to settle in Murphy.'

Not long afterwards, the studbook keeper for cheetahs informed Peter that he could travel to Sweden to collect three young male cheetah brothers, Bajrami, Keene and Martin. This very long journey was carried out by Aaron, one of Peter's grandsons, accompanied by Ian Jones, head of carnivores at Paradise, and Dave the Otter.

After approximately three months of settling in the brothers, Peter agreed to loan Bajrami to Wingham Wildlife Park in Kent, to run with their female cheetah. Soon the very good news for all concerned was the arrival of three cheetah cubs, two males and one female. Sadly, the young female, called Willow, injured her front leg and on the vet's advice she was removed into a separate enclosure for her leg to heal. But when the Wingham team endeavoured to reintroduce Willow back into her family, it sadly became clear that her family would not accept her.

As we have seen, it turned out to be a blessing in disguise. The Wingham team felt Willow's best chance of a good life was for her to be cared for at The Big Cat Sanctuary. Peter and Martin Hill drove over to Wingham to collect her, and she settled in at BCS just as Giles Clark was filming the TV series *Big Cats About the House* for the BBC in which Giles was featured hand-rearing a jaguar cub called Maya. Willow not only found herself welcomed with loving care into a new home, but soon found herself co-starring in the TV series alongside jaguar cub Maya.

It remains an annoying puzzle for Peter as to how his original two cheetahs ended up in Paignton Zoo. But since that perplexing and aggravating non-start, cheetahs have become very much a part of his life. Over several years he has interchanged cheetahs called Pepo, Mephiisto, Mia and Tahnee with Paradise and other collections.

More recently Peter received two male cheetah brothers named Mo and Bolt from Longleat as part of the European Breeding Programme. The plan is for them hopefully to run with Willow. The little cub which was so sadly cast out by her own family has now grown to be a beautiful adult cheetah.

CHAPTER FOURTEEN
Bisa and Zara – Gifts to Uganda

'Peter Sampson has greatly impacted the world. I salute him for the great heart he has, wishing to see everyone happy all the time'
— *Dr James Musinguzi, formerly CEO of the Uganda Wildlife Conservation Education Centre (UWEC), currently Executive Director of Uganda Wildlife Authority (UWA)*

Peter Sampson's contribution to the conservation of endangered big cats is global, perhaps none more significantly so than in Uganda.

Peter first forged links with the East African country in 2008 after being invited to attend a zoo marketing conference in South Africa. He flew first to Johannesburg accompanied by his colleague and good friend Dave the Otter, before they travelled on by road to Pretoria and finally arrived exhausted at a large game reserve. There they queued up along with other delegates to be allocated accommodation for the conference. Some lucky delegates were to be given separate rooms in overnight-stay lodges at the game reserve.

Others not so lucky would be taken to alternative accommodation a bus ride some distance away.

The allocation process was being handled by a female official who was clearly enjoying her designated authority over a line-up of fatigued overseas visitors to decide as to whether they could sleep right there in the game reserve or face a further tiring journey by bus.

Peter and Dave joined the queue and directly in front of them in the line were two men who introduced themselves to the official as Andrew and James from Uganda. 'One of you can stay here,' she barked at the duo, 'but the other one will have to bus it to another lodge.' That was when Peter politely and thoughtfully suggested to the woman that as James and Andrew had travelled a long way together from the same country as part of the same delegation, surely, they should stay in the same lodge together.

'Reluctantly she agreed and handed them the keys,' Peter remembers. 'We were next in line, and she turned to me and said, "I've just given your rooms to them. So, you will have to share a room with your friend." Such is life!' That one considerate act from Peter has, however, led to a long and lasting friendship with both Ugandans.

The following morning Peter attended a presentation by Dr James Musinguzi, CEO of the Uganda Wildlife Conservation Education Centre (UWEC), whom he instantly recognised as the James he had met in the queue for accommodation the night before. During his address Peter was particularly impressed by the efforts Dr Musinguzi was making in the rescue and rehabilitation of wildlife in his eastern part of Africa.

'After my presentation Peter invited me to meet up a for a drink,' Dr Musinguzi recalls. 'He wanted to learn more. I found him to be a passionate soul about wildlife conservation and an ardent lover of cats, and he promised to visit Uganda to see for himself the work our wildlife conservation centre was doing.

'The arrangements were made for Peter to visit, and he subsequently flew out to Uganda with his son Steve. They planned to stay for only one night, but they changed their flights to stay on longer in order to appreciate further and understand more of what we do for wild animals, both on site at UWEC in Entebbe and in the communities.'

On their visit to UWEC, Peter and Steve were introduced to an aged lion which was clearly coming towards the end of its life and, on learning that the number of lions in the wild in Uganda had dwindled to very small numbers, they were prompted to propose a working conservation partnership between UWEC and The Big Cat Sanctuary together with Paradise Wildlife Park.

To cement the new alliance Peter and Steve were invited by Dr Musinguzi to travel with him to Kampala, the capital of Uganda, to meet government ministers and officials for further talks on ways they could together improve conservation. The talks were productive enough for the Ugandans to ask Peter whether they could interest him in setting up a game reserve and a conservation centre for them.

That was a proposal which Peter declared he was prepared to think about. But he was then taken aback when Dr Musinguzi had a further request. He asked Peter if he could send him some lions. Naturally this coals-to-Newcastle request came as a major surprise to Peter. He says, 'My first thoughts were: "Hang on a minute. This is mid-Africa. That's where lions come from. But he is asking me to give him some of my lions." But when I looked back at Uganda's history over recent years, I realised that it wasn't such an unlikely request, and he had every reason to ask. Under the dictator President Idi Amin there had been internal wars and a great many of Uganda's animals had suffered or died through the conflicts. Uganda now had peace – but very few animals. The upshot was that I said yes, I would find lions for him.'

Peter and Steve bid their farewells and flew back to England, formulating plans in their minds to return to Uganda with two healthy lions from Paradise Wildlife Park. As discussions progressed it was agreed that prior to sending any big cats to Uganda, Peter's daughter Lynn and her sons Aaron, Tyler and Cameron, by now much involved in the family business, would fly to Entebbe to meet up with Dr Musinguzi. They needed to satisfy themselves that the living conditions at UWEC would be suitable for the lions they would provide from Paradise and that Uganda possessed the knowledge, the facilities, the keeper experience and the commitment to care for them. Lynn was able to give the Ugandans advice and encouragement, and she also agreed that PWP would finance the building of a new lion enclosure.

Once confident the Ugandans met all the requirements, Peter generously offered to donate two hand-reared lionesses, Bisa and Zara, to become resident at UWEC. Dr Musinguzi was thrilled and profoundly grateful. 'Both had been personally hand-raised by Peter's family, and all arrangements, including permits, were made for them to be flown to Uganda using Peter's resources,' he says. 'It took a year to sort out the paperwork with the Ugandan government, who were understandably anxious to ensure the lionesses they were importing were not carrying any sort of diseases.'

Prior to the arrival of the lionesses, Peter paid for Dr Musinguzi to fly to England to stay as his guest at Paradise. 'I was amazed at Peter's level of hard work,' he says. 'He would wake and be in his office by 5 a.m. every morning.'

For Peter it was an enormous challenge to deliver two lions to Uganda. 'No one had ever sent lions back to Uganda or Africa,' he stresses. 'Sadly, they had only taken them out of Africa. Our Uganda project proved to be extremely difficult from the start. We had to prepare all the paperwork required for this unique transfer and once the documents were in place and the two lions had completed their health checks, we had to plan the actual journey. That was no easy matter as there were no direct flights from the UK to Entebbe. How were we going to convey them 6,000 miles from Hertfordshire to Entebbe? In the end we worked out the best solution would be to transport them by road across the English Channel, on through France, on again through Belgium then on to the Netherlands where we could arrange a flight with KLM from Amsterdam direct to Entebbe airport.'

Peter was reluctant to have the lionesses tranquilised for the journey. Instead, he chose to have them trained for several weeks beforehand so that they would become familiar with the specially constructed crates being used to transport them. This way they would then know something of what to expect in transit. Peter was anxious Bisa and Zara would neither be alarmed by the crates nor regard them as a threat. His priority was to keep them both as calm and as peaceful as possible throughout the entire journey.

The two lionesses left Paradise by road in April 2009 and arrived safely in Amsterdam and without any undue signs of stress. From there their crates were loaded on to a plane and flown to Entebbe before being moved on again by road to UWEC. The whole operation was a great success, and Bisa and Zara were placed first into adjacent enclosures until they were fully acclimatised to their new surroundings, before finally sharing the same home.

For Lynn and her sons, saying goodbye to Zara was a bittersweet moment. They had raised Zara in their own home for the first few months of her life so there was some sadness and tears at her departure as she was like one of the family. But there was joy as well, as they knew she was set for a good new life.

The transfer of the two lionesses to Uganda cost Peter £16,000 and they arrived with a sponsorship package from Peter of £2,000 every year to support Bisa's and Zara's feeding and care. This has recently increased to £3,000 annually and the lionesses have since produced litters of cubs of their own and have contributed immensely to Uganda's conservation education programme.

'Happily, the lions settled into their new home very well after their safe arrival,' Peter enthuses. 'Their transfer was a great achievement, not just for me but for the entire family and, of course, for Uganda. James and his family became, and still are, our very special friends.'

A grateful Dr Musinguzi reports: 'Plans are underway to reintroduce some of the offspring of the lionesses into the wild in Uganda as a research project. And because of our education programme there has been a general appreciation of lions in the country. This has resulted in a slight increase in the number of lions in the wild in Uganda. But the situation is still dire for the lion population. Threats include poisoning by communities for retaliatory killing as a result of lions eating their goats, cows and pigs.'

Peter's working relationship with Uganda was strengthened still further in 2019 when three of his grandsons, Aaron, Tyler and Cameron, embarked on a special trip named Drive4Wildlife in which they drove 4,500 km in just four weeks across Kenya, Tanzania, Rwanda and Uganda to support a range of wildlife charities and organisations in their conservation efforts.

The boys' return after eleven years to UWEC led to them leading a fundraising campaign supported by Paradise and BCS to provide Uganda with a first-ever animal ambulance, a vehicle fully equipped with the latest wildlife protection and rescue modifications. On board is an animal crate to secure rescued animals or to transport any being released back into the wild. The ambulance is equipped with a fridge to store medicines or vaccines and blood samples taken from the field for research purposes. At the front of the vehicle there is a fitted winch if there's a need to pull out any big animals that may have become trapped. Crucially, the ambulance is also equipped with powerful lights to aid night rides for the anti-poaching team.

The ambulance was delivered by the boys as a gift from Peter, the family and the team at both Hertfordshire Zoo and The Big Cat Sanctuary in January 2020 and is currently playing a vital role. The ambulance rescued and rehabilitated 300 animals within the first three years. 'It has been very instrumental in supporting us rescue wild animals from all over Uganda,' says Dr Musinguzi. Peter is exceptionally proud of his grandsons, who have become TV stars in their own right from their five series of *One Zoo Three*, which have included insights into the running of both The Big Cat Sanctuary and Hertfordshire Zoo, and their conservation work in the UK and around the world.

Peter's simple, unprompted act of kindness to two strangers while queuing for a bed for the night thousands of miles from home has in time had an astonishingly beneficial effect on Uganda's wildlife and on the headcount of lions in particular.

Dr Musinguzi says of Peter: 'I learned a lot from him. He's a great and remarkable achiever, an entrepreneur, a motivator, and a generous man with a big heart who above all wishes to see everyone happy. I thank God for his life and the fact that we met.'

As an illustration of Peter's global influence, later that same year he embarked on an action-packed trip to Australia. He was invited to attend the WAZA Directors Conference in Adelaide, Australia, and flew there via Singapore with a stopover specifically timed to enable him to visit both day and night zoos in Singapore and to meet members of their respective teams.

Flying on from the Adelaide conference to Brisbane afforded him the chance to meet up and stay with his great boyhood friend Allen Richardson and his wife Pauline, who arranged a light aircraft flight for him to fly around Fraser Island, then to walk among dingoes and kangaroos and catch sight of dolphins, turtles and sharks.

Then it was back to Brisbane and a visit to Australia Zoo, where he linked up with his good friend and former Paradise Wildlife Park keeper Giles Clark, at that point working as the zoo's senior cat keeper. There, Giles was able to give Peter the opportunity to walk with one of his adult Sumatran tigers. 'And that was very special for me,' Peter says with feeling, 'because sadly this kind of activity is no longer possible in the UK.' Peter's cordial reunion with Giles would have important repercussions, as we saw in Chapter 11.

There was more good news when Dr Musinguzi and his family visited Peter after he sponsored them to stay in the UK for two weeks in June 2023, during which time Dr Musinguzi was an honoured guest at the British and Irish Association of Zoos and Aquarium conference at West Midlands Safari Park along with Lynn and the family. Dr Musinguzi also joined Peter as very special guest speaker at Peter's Dine4Wildlife dinner at Eastwell Manor, Kent, to raise funds and awareness for The Big Cat Sanctuary. The highlight of the Ugandan family's trip was seeing England's national football team play North Macedonia at Manchester United's Old Trafford Stadium – where England won 7-0!

CHAPTER FIFTEEN
Big Cats in Crisis

'Five lions needed rescuing from war-torn Ukraine. There had to be a way'

— *Peter Sampson*

When faced with the human suffering of armed conflicts it can be difficult to think of the parallel impact war has on animals. Historically, the cost of human life has always been the considered priority when two countries go to war. Recognition of, and addressing, the impact of war on animals caught up in conflicts remains largely lacking. Animals are often trapped in the middle of the combat zones with no means of escaping the violence. Traumatised and abandoned, they suffer in silence and in fear.

Such was the desperate plight in 2024 of five lions in Kyiv caught up in Russia's invasion of Ukraine when they came to the attention of Cam Whitnall, Peter's grandson, and Lynn. Learning of their predicament and the distress they had suffered from the ongoing war, Peter and his family felt compelled to act and took the momentous decision to rescue all five and bring them to the safety of The Big Cat Sanctuary where they could give them a permanent home.

A series of meetings assessing the feasibility, logistics, expense, and not least the danger, of a rescue mission eventually led Cam, Peter, Lynn and the team to launch Big Cats in Crisis, a campaign to evacuate the five lions from the Ukraine warzone and give all five a forever home at BCS.

The first funding target was £500,000 to cover the cost of transportation, food and veterinary treatment, and the building of the new Lion Rescue Centre at BCS to accommodate the five with individual indoor dens, each with their own outdoor area.

Remarkably, within three months the fund had reached £311,000 and within five months the total had swollen to £400,500. The first fundraising target was for the rescue from Ukraine to Belgium's Natuurhulpcentrum, Pairi Daiza and Planckendael, which included the transport and also the start of the building of the Big Cats in Crisis rescue centre at BCS by building contractors Scrubs. On 13 November 2024, the £500,000 target was successfully reached thanks to a single £25,000 donation.

The launch of the campaign happened to coincide with Project Lion at BCS, which had been underway for several months with the aim of enhancing the living conditions for the sanctuary's existing pride and to accommodate additional lions. The urgent Ukraine appeal accelerated the team's efforts to build the additional indoor and outdoor rescue facilities.

The five lions which Peter and his family volunteered to rescue and rehome comprised of one male named Rori and four lionesses, Amani, Lira, Vanda and Yuna. Each had been found abandoned in various locations in Donetsk and Luhansk, two of the areas worst hit by the Russian invasion of Ukraine. Prior to the war, they were kept in private homes – a house, a flat, garden sheds – from the illegal wildlife trade. As citizens fled the devastation of the war, the lions were left helpless, scared, neglected and then abandoned while their surroundings came under bombardment.

Most of the five were suffering from post-traumatic stress disorder (PTSD) and all five were in some distress, having endured the terrible noise, chaos and destruction caused by Russian missiles and drone attacks exploding around them.

Yuna had been discovered near Kyiv living alongside a male lion named

Atlas in a cramped 4×4 metre enclosure with bare concrete for flooring. The two illegally bred cats, both approximately three years old, had been abandoned by their owner, who had fled when Atlas became aggressive during the heavy Russian shelling of Kyiv.

Of the five lions requiring rescue, Yuna was in the worst condition.

Malnourished, she was found to have extensive wounds and to be suffering from severe concussion and shellshock. She had been traumatised after debris from a missile attack landed 300 metres from their enclosure and she had been experiencing symptoms of ataxia and vestibular syndrome, which left her with coordination problems and struggling to walk or even stand.

Rori was discovered alone in a private home which had been abandoned in January 2023 due to the Russian invasion. Like Yuna, he was suffering from shellshock and for two weeks was unable to stand until he had received intensive rehabilitation.

Lioness Vanda was found by a member of the Ukrainian military in February 2024, cooped up in a small apartment building near the front line. It was thought that she had been kept in the apartment for six months without any outdoor access or sunlight and had been raised on an inappropriate diet. She was infested with parasites and was displaying signs of rickets.

There was better news about the remaining two lionesses, Amani and Lira, earmarked for transfer to BCS. They were found to be sisters and, although they were thought to have been illegally bred for photo exploitation, they appeared to be fit and healthy.

Quite apart from the dangers of such a rescue mission, the logistics of evacuating the lions across six different countries to BCS represented a massive challenge.

Working alongside the International Fund for Animal Welfare (IFAW), Peter's stated mission was firstly to have the five lions transported from the war zones to the temporary safety of the Wild Animal Rescue (WAR) centre near Kyiv and held there while he built his rescue centre at The Big Cat Sanctuary to accommodate them. The five would then be transported 1,400 miles to BCS, where they would be welcomed and permanently cared for till the end of their days.

The family's generous offer to give these five lions a permanent home at Smarden in the peace of the Kent countryside was welcomed with open arms by WAR's Natalia Popova, who had spent time on the front lines rescuing animals. 'I'm so relieved they now have a much better life ahead,' she said. 'It's a scary time for everyone in Ukraine, and these big cats must have been so frightened and confused – some were born during the conflict and knew no life other than the constant noise and chaos of war.'

On the afternoon of Wednesday 14 August 2024, Yuna and Rori were crated up at the Wild Animals Rescue Centre in Kyiv and taken to the Natuurhulpcentrum in Belgium as the first practical steps in the rescue mission.

At one point the project appeared to be doomed to failure. It was a race against time but, to the consternation of Cam and his team, they discovered the law required for the lions to be placed in quarantine for four months before the cats could be cleared for life in the UK. Fortunately, each of the lions had been in isolation for a year anyway, so the quarantine was eventually waived.

Yuna was the first of the five scheduled to arrive at BCS. A rescue team was assembled headed by Cam and it took many meetings both inside and outside the boardroom before Yuna's evacuation plan was given the go-ahead.

Along with Rori, Yuna was collected from the WAR centre on the afternoon of Wednesday 14 August, and driven by Geert, a true legend from Cross Border Animal Services (CBAS), more than 2,000 km on a journey lasting the best part of two days to the Natuurhulpcentrum animal shelter in Oudsbergen, Belgium. Here Rori would be unloaded to be given a temporary home while Yuna headed for the UK.

The biggest challenge along the way was the border crossing between Ukraine and Poland, where there was some uncertainty as to whether Yuna and Rori would be allowed entry into the EU. The news that they had successfully entered Poland was the signal for project leader Cam and BCS curator Briony Smith to prepare to travel from Smarden via the Eurotunnel to France and then on to Oudsbergen to meet up with Yuna for her ten-hour journey to her new BCS home.

The lioness arrived in the middle of the night and Cam was able to inform Peter that the first part of his five-lion Ukraine rescue project had been safely accomplished. 'Yuna was surprisingly calm when we got to BCS,' Briony assured Peter, 'and she came out of her crate and into her bedroom like an angel. She seems already to be grateful for the peace and quiet of BCS.'

Yuna naturally was at first cautious of her unfamiliar surroundings and spent a lot of time sleeping and resting before gradually building up confidence in her new environment.

Within forty-eight hours she was curious enough to leave the shelter of her den to explore her outdoor area. Cam and the team watched heart in mouth as Yuna tentatively padded out and up on to a grassy mound, mindful that every step she took was brand new. Having spent her entire life with concrete underfoot, now for the first time she was experiencing the feel of her paws on grass.

For Peter, seeing Yuna walk on grass was an extraordinary déjà vu moment. It took him back exactly forty years, when, following his purchase of the old Broxbourne Zoo, he had built a new enclosure for Bobby, his very first lion, and had watched with immense satisfaction as Bobby left his new den to tread, like Yuna, on grass for the very first time.

Now, four decades on, history had repeated itself in the most unlikely but heart-warming way.

Structural building work on the BCS rescue centre neared completion at the end of 2024, and with landscaping expected to finish early in 2025 the remaining four lions were on schedule to arrive from Ukraine within weeks. Peter, Lynn, Cam and the team were ready to give them a life-changing welcome and a forever home.

In many ways, this was just the beginning. As the gates to the Lion Rescue Centre were officially opened on 25th March 2025 by Cam, Peter, Lynn, Paul Hollywood (Ambassador), General Valerii Zaluzhnyi (the Ukrainian Ambassador to the UK and Head of the Ukraine Army) and Baroness Hayman (Under-Secretary of State for the environment at DEFRA), the world watched these incredible lions take their first steps into a life of safety, care and dignity.

For Rori, Vanda, Amani, and Lira, their harrowing journey from a war-torn country to the peaceful sanctuary of Kent was finally over. No longer just survivors, they were now symbols of hope, resilience and the unwavering dedication of those who fought to give them a future.

As Cam and the team stood back, watching the lions explore their new home, there was a quiet sense of triumph. The rescue had been a success not just for these lions, but for every animal that would follow in their footsteps.

The story of the Lion Rescue Centre wasn't just about one mission; it was about setting a new standard for rescue, conservation, and care. And with that, The Big Cat Sanctuary looks forward to the next rescue, the next life saved, and the next chance to make a positive impact in the world, one cat at a time.

CHAPTER SIXTEEN
A Myriad of Memories and Magical Moments

Peter Sampson takes a personal look back with Tim Ewbank on the people, places, friendships and events that have enriched his life.

The Loan Ranger

Over the years I made regular visits with Rachael to Dartmoor Zoo. We became good friends with the owner Ellis Daw and we exchanged various animals. On one particular visit to collect a young jaguar cub, Ares, that had been rejected by its mother, Ellis revealed that the local authority would not be renewing his zoo licence.

To be fair, this was understandable. Ellis had built a modern, up-to-date zoo, but time and lack of maintenance had taken its toll and the local authority had placed various conditions on the renewal to meet new zoo standards.

Their requirements were justified, but Ellis objected to such an extent that he even had a coffin placed in reception with the licensing officer's name on it. Not the greatest idea.

Without a licence the zoo faced closure, but there were animals still to feed and staff to pay. Desperate for money, Ellis decided to sell the zoo but asked me for a £20,000 loan to keep it running until the sale went through – and I agreed. On our journey home with the young jaguar, Ares, Rachael said she doubted whether I'd ever see that money again.

A few weeks later we travelled back to Dartmoor Zoo once more to see how the sale was progressing whereupon Ellis asked if I would be interested in buying his zoo but at half the asking price.

It was a generous offer but a step too far for me while I was developing Paradise Wildlife Park and The Big Cat Sanctuary at the same time. Happily, Ellis managed to sell Dartmoor Zoo to a gentleman named Ben Mee who has worked hard to build it into the excellent zoo it is today. Happily, too, Ellis was as good as his word and paid me back my loan in full.

My memory of Ellis is a little old man in a woolly hat. No one would ever have guessed that earlier in his life he was the world stock-car champion.

My Pride

My grandson Cameron was one of twenty-six young environmentalists to be invited by Prime Minister Boris Johnson to represent the UK government at COP26 in Glasgow. Cam presented live throughout the event and gave a presentation on biodiversity.

My daughter Lynn carried the baton for the Commonwealth Games in Birmingham. She carried it around the white-water rafting centre at Lea Valley and had the challenge of being strapped into a boat to ride the rapids.

I was asked to write a report for parliamentary review backed by Lord Pickles, Lord Blunkett and Michael Gove MP. The report was to highlight both our charities The Zoological Society of Hertfordshire, now Hertfordshire Zoo and The Big Cat Sanctuary, what we had achieved and committed to conservation both in the UK and worldwide, and our achievements in our European breeding programmes and sit on committees for our wildlife associations.

Members of our teams from both charities are represented on various breeding programmes and panels.

On average, the conservation cabin at Hertfordshire Zoo raises £100,000 a year for various conservation projects worldwide. Operating for over twenty years, it was started by Lynn, Pia Gismondi and the late Karen Barrington, with Barbara Turner currently heading up the volunteer team as well as the thousands of pounds donated to conservation projects and good causes, plus equipment and time over each year.

Earning my Stripes

The trustees of both charities, Hertfordshire Zoo and The Big Cat Sanctuary, have set up the Peter Sampson Award. Up to £10,000 can be awarded to assist other charities for emergency and disaster appeals, as well as the thousands of pounds donated to conservation projects and good causes, plus equipment and time over the years.

Racing Around

Part of my membership and licensing role for BIAZA was to check on animal welfare standards at existing member zoos. How fortunate for me that my inspection of Curraghs Wildlife Park in the Isle of Man happened to coincide with the isle's famous TT races. I carried out the zoo inspection with my dear friend, the late vet John Lewis, like me a motorbike fan. Two others from Paradise with a great love of motorbikes, Steve Saunders and Mick Lewis, also joined us for four fabulous days.

Hoddesdon With Love

My hometown, Hoddesdon, has its own special committee called Love Hoddesdon organised by Stephen Harris. At Christmas, we supply our large pickup truck for the festive parade. It was driven for many years by one of our team, the late Big Steve Hughes, acting as Father Christmas. My grandsons Aaron, Tyler and Cameron have given three live performances at the Spotlight Theatre of their popular *One Zoo Three* TV show. It was also a privilege for my grandsons to turn on the Hoddesdon Christmas lights.

Doubling Up – An Exciting Future

Paradise Wildlife Park started out as a 32-acre site. Now, thanks to three new recent purchases of land, Hertfordshire Zoo has expanded to 65 acres, room for development by Lynn and my grandsons and for the addition of different species of larger animals in the years to come.

Under Arrest

One bright and sunny morning back in my coach and bus days, a police car pulled into my new Brimsdown coach depot in north London. Two police officers entered the building and I went downstairs from my office to meet them only to find I was being put under arrest. But it wasn't a fair cop. In collusion with my members of staff it was just a set-up, a big joke that ended in laughter all round.

The real reason for the visit was that Phil Buckland, one of the officers, was the proud owner of two vintage double-decker buses and he possessed a PSV licence to drive coaches. For many years thereafter he regularly drove Sampson coaches on his days off.

One year he entered his ex-London transport red double-decker bus for a coach rally in the north of England. Along with Phil's wife Scovula, Rachael and I joined a group of friends on the long bus journey north, taking it in turns to drive over the Pennines. I was the driver to take the bus up the M1 to Manchester and then on to Harrogate, stopping at Harry Ramsden's fish and chip shop on the way.

The rally was a two-day event involving more than a hundred buses and coaches and Phil's red bus was voted the top bus in all classes, resulting in us receiving a very shiny trophy.

Phil and Scovula became great friends of ours. He was something of a historian and had studied books on World War I. His knowledge proved invaluable as a tour guide when Rachael organised visits to France and Belgium for a tour of the war graves.

Inspirational Molly

The late Molly Badham was an inspiration. Sadly, our good friend Molly has passed away, but it was Molly and Nat that had built Twycross Zoo in the Midlands over many years and it was without doubt a world-class zoo. Myself and Rachael travelled to Twycross, as I was invited to speak as a tribute to Molly about her life and legacy. For me, it was a great privilege to speak about not only a good friend, but a wonderful person. My good friend Dominique Tropeano from Colchester Zoo joined me as we paid tribute to Molly.

The Arrival of Palm Civets

Along with Ken Sims, who owned Thrigby Hall Wildlife Park near Great Yarmouth, and Stewart Muir from Newquay Zoo, we decided to bring three pairs of Owston's palm civets into the country. This proved very successful. Our major claim to fame here at Paradise was that we were the first zoo in the UK to breed them.

Ain't Life Grand?

Rachael's first grandson, Jayden, was born and her first granddaughter, Lily, followed soon afterwards. In time a second granddaughter arrived, called Summer. A very special time in our lives.

Motherly Love

During the Paradise Wildlife Park days, Lynn and the team built a new small coffee shop near the World of Dinosaurs. Lynn named it Grace's Coffee, after her mum, and it has proved to be a great addition.

A Willing Friend

Vic Cooper, a long term friend, installed our luxury overnight stay lodges at The Big Cat Sanctuary, and then invited me fly to Gambia, where we explored the possibility of establishing a small sanctuary. Vic had a very large parcel of land in Gambia, upon which he had started to develop and had built accommodation for himself. Vic very generously revealed that he would like to bequeath in his will his land and what was on it to The Big Cat Sanctuary.

Bella

After the loss of our much-loved domestic cat Purdy on the same day as Rocky, our tiger, Rachael decided we should have a small dog. We elected to have a King Charles spaniel and eventually found a breeder in Camberley, Surrey.

On our arrival we were introduced to five pups. Rachael immediately warmed to one female pup and we both agreed she was the one for us. She's called Bella, and she's a great little friend to us both and to all the team at Hertfordshire Zoo.

Sun Bears

One of the largest developments we carried out at Paradise was the creation of Sun Bear Heights, which incorporated a new area for binturong and Asian short-clawed otters, and a new house and enclosure for our jaguars. It prompted a visit and a fascinating talk and presentation to team members and guests about sun bears by Dr Wong. Around the same time, we held our Summer Ball here at Hertfordshire Zoo and the funds raised were donated to Dr Wong and the new sun bear release centre in Borneo.

The Change of Power!

Looking back in history, when I operated our bus and coach business, I converted two of our large coaches which had petrol engines, I replaced them after a great deal of work, cutting and shutting with the more powerful diesel engines. How things have changed over that time. John Ashburner a member of our team at Hertfordshire Zoo has recently undertaken the conversion and welding work to do the reverse that I had undertaken all those years ago. We had two railway engines pulling carriages on what we call our Rex Express train on our dinosaur railway, both were powered by diesel engines, over the past few months with John's hard work and dedication, John has removed the diesel engines and replaced them with electric motors which are battery powered. This has proved to be very successful but also a big improvement to our environment.

Israel and the EAZA Zoo Conference

I travelled to Jerusalem with Bob Lawrence from West Midlands Safari Park. It proved a great opportunity to meet up with zoo colleagues from all over Europe. Jerusalem, without doubt, is a very special place and I felt privileged to be there. I can recall myself and Bob swimming, or should I say floating, in the Black Sea. We visited the Wailing Wall and had the opportunity to pay our respects. On several evenings, we dined with our Jewish friends. We also opted to cross the border into the Arab community to meet and dine with them. It was a great experience.

To Visit Portugal and the Algarve

I was invited to Portugal by my friend Andy Mahoney, whom I have known for many years, dating as far back as the speedway and coaching days. Andy had built up a large business transporting children and adults with disabilities. Andy had purchased a small hotel in Portugal where he was busy converting the bedrooms to accommodate his guests with disabilities. Andy wanted to have a small petting zoo within the grounds of the hotel, hence the reason for my visit, to help and plan the enclosures and to see what animals would be suitable. I have since visited Andy and Portugal several times. Andy has now established a first-class facility.

Acknowledgements

By Peter Sampson

I wish to express my sincere thanks to all the staff, colleagues, volunteers and friends, both past and present, for their support and for all their hard work. Without their much-valued contributions to The Big Cat Sanctuary and Hertfordshire Zoo (formally Paradise Wildlife Park), the homes for the animals in our care wouldn't be what they are today.

The list of people I'd like to thank for helping me to achieve my aims in breeding and conservation is endless. It is far too long to mention everyone individually, but special thanks must go to Rachael, my long-term partner, and her family for their unfailing support for all I do. To my daughter Lynn and my son Steve, both of whom willingly supported me in my original decision to step into the unknown and buy the desperately rundown Broxbourne Zoo forty years ago. Their constant support has been invaluable. Special thanks are also due to Grace, who stood by me when I had previously taken an equally uncertain step into the world of speedway, then into the bus and coach travel business.

In more recent times, my grandsons, Aaron, Tyler and Cameron, who have and still are achieving so much in the animal and conservation world. Also, my grandson Scott, who is serving as a chef in the Welsh Guards Regiment of the British Army, not forgetting Carly and my great-grandson Alfie, who hopefully will be following in the family's footsteps for many years to come.

About Tim Ewbank

Tim Ewbank is a former Fleet Street journalist and author of best-selling biographies, including of David Jason, Rod Stewart and Joanna Lumley.

Tim was motivated to write this book after a chance introduction to Peter Sampson, followed by a visit to the Big Cat Sanctuary, where he was further inspired to chronicle Peter's extraordinary passion for the conservation of big cats.

Peter's enthusiasm echoed in some measure a similar passion for big cats shown to Tim by his own father, Harry Ewbank, who reared two small tiger cubs while stationed in the army in India. On leaving the military, Harry became a member of London Zoo, and on subsequent retirement from his life as a teacher, spent numerous days at the zoo photographing, painting, or simply quietly observing the tigers he loved. Tim dedicates this book to him, and also to Maike, for her love, support and encouragement.

About Hertfordshire Zoo and The Big Cat Sanctuary

Hertfordshire Zoo (charity no. 1108609), formerly known as Paradise Wildlife Park, is set in the beautiful surroundings of Broxbourne Woods in the heart of the Hertfordshire countryside. The zoo is home to a wide range of animals, from lions and lemurs to snakes to otters, and has celebrated forty-one years of breeding and conservation. The zoo recently opened their Lions of India, the Asiatic lions from the Gir forest region.

The Big Cat Sanctuary (charity no. 1104420) in Kent is a charity dedicated to the welfare and conservation of wild cats, both large and small. Spanning 32 acres, the sanctuary offers species-specific enclosures, a cutting-edge veterinary centre and first-class facilities designed to meet the unique needs of its feline residents.

For more information, and to become a member, please scan the below QR code.

www.ingramcontent.com/pod-product-compliance
Lightning Source LLC
Chambersburg PA
CBHW061229070526
44584CB00030B/4053